THE ETRL

A STORY ABOUT HOW ONE MAN
TRANSFORMED AN EMPIRE

Rome has a deep past that leans heavily upon what came before it, the Etruscans. This story tells how one man's life helped transform Rome into *The Eternal City*. There would be no Rome unless, first, you had the Etruscans.

Julian Di Donato

ACKNOWLEDGMENTS

I would first like to acknowledge the foundation of this book, *The Parallel Lives by Plutarch,* published in Vol. II of the Loeb Classical Library Edition 1914, *The Life of Camillus.* Although the timing of events in the novel has been consolidated, the historical background is based on the vast information Plutarch recorded centuries ago. Without continually referencing his work, the characters and storyline of this novel could not have been written.

I would also like to acknowledge the contributions of The Penn Museum Volume 27 Issue 2. It was initially published in 1985, Etruscan Athletics, *Glimpse of an Elusive Civilization,* by Karen Brown Vellucci. Her study of the Etruscan archaeological sites at Poggio Civitate revealed insights into the patterns of Etruscan life, especially their

1

athletic and competitive endeavors during the fourth century BC. Her work was the inspiration behind many of the characters in this book.

A substantial portion of the information concerning the daily life of the Etruscan people was generously supplied by The Journal of the Etruscan Foundation, Etruscan Studies, Volume 9, Article 14, 2002, *Servants at a Rich Man's Feast; Early Etruscan Household Slaves and Their Procurement*, by Daphine Nash Briggs. Her descriptions involving mining, crafts, garments, textiles, household economy, servants, slaves, feasts, wedding customs, riding, and even theft and kidnapping, can be attributed to her informative and comprehensive work.

I would also like to cite the Academic Dictionaries and Encyclopedia and Wikipedia for their use in researching the life of Marcus Furius Camillus and the positions of Dictator and Military Tribunes and for providing insights into the impact of the Gauls upon the Etruscans and Roman civilizations.

My grasp of what it was like to be an Etruscan some 2,400 years ago was first obtained from reading Joaques

Heorgon's book, Daily Life of the Etruscans, The Macmillan Company New York, 1964. The information about every aspect of the Etruscan culture was extensive; their religion, family, work, play, clothing, luxuries, food, banquets, music, and entertainment were described in detail. I was able to bring my characters to life in a more accurate and complete setting by referring to his work.

Finally, I want to thank my editor, Trudy Higgins. Her skills vastly improved this book.

Thank you, Trudy.

DEDICATION

This book is dedicated to the Etruscan people. We are still in the early stages of learning about them, who they were, where they came from, and how they lived. But some things are becoming clear. They developed their unique skills, art, and culture over centuries, inspired by the many Mediterranean cultures surrounding them, and have altered the path of western civilization more than is assumed. We owe considerable debt to this mysterious and wondrous culture.

If your DNA holds genes derived, even partially, from populations based on the Italian peninsula, you are carrying on their legacy.

TABLE OF CONTENTS

CHAPTER 1: I AM TOSCANO

Remember, Nico, aim your spear at its throat, and the moment it's in range, strike with all your might

I'm scared, Toscano.

I was scared at my dawning, also, but your instincts will take over once the boar gets close. You won't be able to think of anything else. Nico, the strength is within you, and I'll be beside you. Are you ready, my brother?

Yes, I'm ready.

Good. We'll know the time is near when we hear the yelling of the hunting party.

I hear them.

There he is! Now Nico! Now! You did it. I'm so proud of you.

Toscano, you're bleeding.

I'm fine; it's only......

Toscano? Toscano? Help! It's Toscano. He's bleeding. It won't stop.

Cave of the Shaman

I slowly drifted above a vast forest. A gentle breeze flowed around me. I could feel the sun warming my face. In the distance, I could see mountains rising ahead of me. As they grew closer, I began to descend gradually. I could see a cave through an opening in the trees. It looked familiar. It was the Cave of the Shaman. I was being drawn deep inside.

The next moment I was lying on the Shaman's altar. The walls were spinning with flaming torches circling me. Flashes of images began racing through my head. I reached out to my parents and brother, but they soon faded away, and I could not touch them. I was lying there still, unable to move or make a sound as I drifted between this world and the next.

Forcing my eyes open, I could see the cave was filled with smoke and saturated with the smell of incense. I began to sense my body and tried to sit up, but I still could barely move. Glancing down towards my waist, I could see it was covered with thick wrapping, and I saw standing beside me was the Shaman. Only her outline was visible as an enormous fire raged behind her. She was deep in a trance, swaying endlessly, chanting, and waving offerings above me, imploring the gods to bring me back to life.

Moments later, I felt her hand slip beneath my neck, gently lifting my head to drink as she whispered, *"here, my child, drink slowly, soon your strength shall return. The gods are strong within you, my son. They have heard my prayers and have brought you back among the living. They speak to me loudly; a grand destiny lies before you."* Still weak and barely able to move, I looked into her eyes, not knowing what to make of what she said, and slowly took a sip.

She gently laid my head back down, and I soon drifted into a deep sleep.

When I awoke again, now standing beside me was Lord Acri.

I heard what you did at the dawning, Toscano. You're lucky to be alive; raging boars are usually deadly.

You do what you must to protect your family, my lord.

Shaman Alysa tells me you have only survived because the gods wish you to live. But the gods aren't the only ones that feel this way, Toscano.

Thank you, my lord.

See me when your strength returns. I have plans for you that we need to discuss.

I will, my lord.

Your family is anxious to see you. I will have them come in.

Thank you, my lord.

Toscano, my son, praise to the gods, you're alive. We thought you were joining the dead. Glory to the gods, for they have willed you to live, my son.

Yes, they must have, mother, petitioned by your prayers and those of Alysa; I live once more.

Toscano, I thought you were about to die.

I'm fine, little brother, and it'll take more than a wild boar to kill me. I am Toscano.

Home of Toscano

Toscano, now that you have regained your strength, my son, it is time for the hunt.

Can Nico join me this season, father?

Do you think he's ready?

He is, I'm sure of it. He showed remarkable bravery at his dawning.

From what I recall, it was you who showed the bravery of a warrior that day.

Nico proved it's within him also. He's ready, father. Plus, I can use the help carrying back the huge roebuck we'll be bringing down.

Please, father, let me go with Nico.

Mother, what do you think?

Knowing our boys, I don't think there'll be any talking them out of it now that they've decided.

If that is what you both wish. Go, and good luck on your hunt. But just in case that huge roebuck eludes you, don't come back empty-handed. Bring back a load of green ore on your return. Our lord is asking for more weapons.

Father, mother, before I go, I must speak about something to both of you.

What is it, my son?

King Acri called me for an audience. He has asked me to lead his militia.

Lead his militia? When was this?

He asked me to see him as soon as I was able. You know it's right for me, father. But before I give him my answer, I would like your blessing and mother's.

Are you sure you want to do this? This is so sudden, my son.

You know it is father, from when I was a young boy and first saw the matches with you at Fanum Voltumnae.

Toscano, you had shown me from when you were a young boy that you knew what you truly desired for your life. I will not stand in your way now. You have my blessing, my son.

Mother, do I have your blessings also?

Are you sure of this, Toscano?

I know it's my destiny, mother; it is what I must do.

You have always shown the courage of a warrior, even as a young boy, Toscano. You were always the first to stand up to someone when needed. Courage runs deep in you, my son. If you feel this is what you must do, you have my blessing also. But Toscano, promise me you will always use your wisdom combined with your courage. Combining both will make you the strongest of warriors and help to keep you safe

I will, mother; you have my word.

Enough of this talk now. Go and bring me back that ore.

You will have both meat and ore, father, in a few days.

Nico, come on, we have a long hunt ahead of us, and it's time we are on our way. Your mother has fed you enough.

May the gods be with you, my sons.

Entering The Lemon Forest

I know this path you are taking, Toscano.

Oh, you do.

Yes, won't this path take us by the village of Brescia? Just a guess.

It will, my brother. It's the more scenic route.

Ah, yes, the longer, more scenic route. And one that happens to pass by the exact scene you desire.

A slightly longer route sometimes has its rewards, brother. Someday soon, you will understand.

Oh, that day has already passed, my brother.

Village of Brescia

Gia, look who is approaching. I do believe it's your suitor, Toscano. And look, he brings a companion for me.

Vera, why don't you bring this flour inside to mother?

And miss my chance to meet my future husband. Oh no, I'm staying right here at the millstone with you.

Vera, please, give me a private moment with Toscano and bring this flour inside.

Ugh, I am just too kind to you, sister.

You are most kind, Vera; thank you. Now go.

Nico, why don't you go check out that sow over there? We may want to trade for it at the harvest festival. It looks like it'll feed us for the entire winter.

Indeed, my brother, I'll gladly allow you to visit with your fair maiden and undoubtedly enjoy getting acquainted with that pig. And I don't even speak pig!

Oh yes, you do. I hear you snoring like one every night.

Toscano, so good to see you. I see you're traveling with a companion.

Yes, he's my brother, Nico. He's doing a little sow shopping right now.

She is a prize. My father expects she will bring in a small fortune at this year's festival.

And he usually does get his way.

He does.

Gia, I am sure my father would be honored to have your family as our guests for dinner after the trading.

I am sure my father will be honored to accept.

Gia, we need to talk. But not now, later, in the village when we can get a chance to be alone.

I will make sure we get that chance, Toscano.

14

I must be going. It looks like Nico has lost interest in your sow.

Goodbye, Toscano, and good fortune on your hunt.

Goodbye, Gia, we'll see each other soon.

Yes, we will.

Well, was your scenic detour a success?

Time will tell. Let's get on with our hunt and keep up with me, little brother.

The Lemon Forest

Toscano, I want to join the militia like you when I am older.

Nico, there's plenty of time before you'll need to decide on something like that.

But I know already.

If that is the life you shall choose, I will be honored to have you with me. Now, the less we talk, the better if we ever want to get in range of a roebuck.

Toscano, it's been two days roaming this forest, and the largest animal we've seen is that black squirrel over there.

Quiet Nico, look there, beside that out-cropping.

I see it, and it looks well out of range, even for you, Toscano.

Don't move.

Toscano, you downed it!

No, it's not down, not yet. It wasn't a kill shot. Let's go quickly. We must track him down before it gets away.

We've lost it, Toscano.

No, over here, look, fresh blood. Let's go— this way.

Toscano, there, just beyond those two trees.

I see him.

Look at those antlers. He's huge. Finish him, Toscano.

What was that?

Another strike. Someone else has just taken down our roebuck.

Stop, back away. This roebuck is mine. I downed him.

Yes, and a fine strike it was, but as you can see, it was not the first.

But it was the strike that brought him down. So, it's mine.

Your strike may have brought him down, but he was already bleeding out and would have fallen soon.

16

Well, I made it so. This roebuck is mine. I have many mouths to feed, and a storm will soon be upon us.

I also can make that claim, with many waiting for this meat upon our return.

Hold on, the both of you. The roebuck is big enough to share and will be less of a load for each if we do. The both of you agree to split the kill, or I will watch you fight to the death and take all the spoils myself. I have no problem bragging about how I brought down my first roebuck.

You are wise beyond your years, my brother. Do you agree, stranger? Do we split the kill?

It's agreed, but the rack is mine.

Hold on; you two can draw lots for it and keep this all fair.

Clever brother, how about it, stranger? Are you feeling lucky today?

I am. I'm having a run of good luck today.

Well, it does look like you are the lucky one. Congratulations. Now Nico, take my blade and let's see if you are as good at butchering as you are at making deals. What do they call you, stranger?

My name is Matteo, and you?

I'm Toscano, and this is my younger brother Nico. Have you traveled far for this kill?

It's been days, and you? Where are you two from?

We've been traveling from the north on the sixth day of our hunt.

That's a long hunt for one roebuck.

Yes, but now a successful one. You're a talented hunter. I admire your skill with that bow, Matteo.

Some say I am. It will be dark soon, and now that our business is done, it is time for me to be on my way. Safe travels to you both.

May the gods' speed be with you, Matteo, and have a safe return to your village.

Six days from the north? Why were you trying to deceive him, Toscano?

Did you take note of his skill with that bow? That strike pieced the chest right into the heart. And how he managed that knife; he butchered his half of that roebuck as quickly and cleanly as I have ever seen. And his weapons, did you notice that dagger and battle-ax beneath his waistcoat? Those are not usually weapons of a hunter.

True, very observant, my brother.

Better we misdirect him to our destination than take the chance of leading him straight to our village. He could be scouting for a new target to raid. Now, let's go and put some miles between us before dark. We have at least a three-day journey before reaching the copper mines to dig out that ore for father.

CHAPTER 2: THE BANISHED ONE

Nico, let's stop here and set camp for the night.

Fine with me, my brother. I'll gather some dry tinder for the fire.

No, hold on for a moment. I must tell you something first. We're being followed.

I didn't see anyone.

I heard something about an hour ago. I wasn't sure at first, but I heard it again just after crossing that stream. It sounds like the footsteps of someone trailing about twenty paces behind us.

Let's turn back and see who it is.

I am sure it's our hunting friend we just met. I'm going to circle back and surprise him.

I want to go with you.

No, I want you to stay here and start to make camp. You'll be a distraction until I can come up behind him.

Suppose you're not back within twenty minutes. I'm coming after you.

It'll be back sooner than that.

Be careful.

I headed to the east, away from the camp, then slowly turned north, moving silently through the thick underbrush, circling to come up behind him. Judging from the footsteps I heard, I was confident that it was only one person, and it must be our new hunting competitor, Matteo.

It wasn't long before I spotted him, just as I suspected, about forty paces before me. He must have started following us right after we parted. It all made sense; besides his weapons, he wore more skins and furs than someone out on a local hunt. And judging by the wear on his clothing, he's been traveling for weeks. When I was close enough, I stood up and openly called out to him, letting him know it was me and not something else for him to kill. He quickly turned towards me with his bow drawn, ready to strike.

Oh, hold on there, it's me, Matteo, Toscano. Can you calmly put down that bow and tell me why you're following us?

You are lucky you don't have an arrow between your ribs coming up behind me like that.

Why don't you tell me why you're following us?

I don't have a reason exactly. Honestly, my curiosity about you two got the best of me. I was about to break off and head on my way when I noticed you altering direction and heading more south. The further south you traveled, the more curious I became.

Curious? About us? Well, I'm just as curious about you. You're not just on a hunt, are you? You're not some ordinary hunter.

I only hunt when I need to eat to survive.

It looks like you've been out here for some time, Matteo. Your clothing and weapons give you away. You're a scout, or you have been banished from somewhere. And it's been for a long while. Isn't that right, Matteo?

You're a keen observer, my friend. I have been traveling for months, and it's a long story. Darkness is about to close us in. Why don't we continue this over a fire at your camp, and we'll learn about each?

Fine, join us before my brother eats all our venison.

Approaching Camp

21

Nico, it is me, and I brought company.

I see. Matteo, why are you acting so shy? If you wanted our company, you just had to ask.

You two are curious fellows. I thought it best to stay cautious.

Nico, how is that venison coming?

It is about ready.

Good, our friend here and I are starving, and he promised to tell us why we found him wandering around in this forest in the first place.

You will hear my story, but first, you must promise to be as forthcoming about yourselves.

Nico, give our guest the first cut. He needs to build his energy for all he is about to tell us. This is going to be an informative evening for all of us.

So, now, Matteo, tell us how you ended up a nomad roaming the Lemon Forest.

I'm not sure this one night will be long enough to tell it all.

Go ahead and begin. We can always finish it with wine when we return home. You are to be our guest.

Well, that is kind of you, Toscano. I guess the best place to start is at the very beginning. I was born into a family of four with an older brother, Janus, in our village, back in Vacalvi. Our ruler had decreed that the first-born male of a family was to learn his father's trade and continue the family livelihood upon his passing. If there were a second male child, he would be required to enter the warrior training school during his fifth year.

Having a son become a warrior was a great honor for a family and earned the respect of the entire village. So, soon after my fifth birthday, I began. My parents were proud of me even at that early age. They saw that I had the physical skill and strength well beyond what was needed to follow the leathercrafting trade of my father. If I remember correctly, more than a few that first year were dismissed early on. They were either too weak or sickly to keep up with the rest of us. Those first years, we gathered at the village courtyard early each morning. I remember we were all very eager. Our teacher, Horace, was firm but kind to us. We all enjoyed what we were being taught. At first, we thought we were playing games, but later we knew they all had a purpose. They were the foundation of the trade; we were committing to becoming warriors for the rest of our lives.

It started with wrestling. Horace would show us how to maintain balance and read our opponents, searching and testing for weaknesses. We learned quickly, and soon he taught different holds, throw downs, and move combinations. I excelled at wrestling and advanced rapidly. I could not wait to get home and try what I had learned with my older brother, Janus. I soon passed him in skill, and he refused to wrestle me any longer.

We were fed well those days, with meals of meat, seasonal crops, and bread after each session. Those meals were among the absolute best I've had to this day. Most days, I would ask to bring home a second helping, giving it to my mother. She would add it to our family meal that evening, turning it into a real feast.

By our third year, we were already developing the strength and muscle of skilled athletes much stronger than the older children. We all felt proud to be part of this elite group. We moved on to using mock weapons in our fourth year of training. I guarded my first shield and wooden sword with my life, keeping them by my bedside each night throughout my apprenticeship. When we were nine or ten, our teacher started to enforce more discipline, and the training slowly became more rigorous. The competition among us also increased. During my twelfth year, we moved on to actual weapons. First was the hunting bow. I remember watching the craftsman fashioning my bow. He was named Nerie. It took weeks of work before it was finished. He custom-made it to match my size and growing strength. It was perfect. Whenever I could, I would go and watch him make it. He would wet and bind various wood species to form the curve and obtain his desired flex. Next was the string. He twisted strands of linen and hemp together until he felt it had the proper stretch and strength to withstand even my strongest pull. He took extreme pride in his work and was not satisfied until he felt the bow was flawless. He finished it by engraving the words ``Property of Matteo Di Vacalvi" to the bottom limb and added my mark of the wolf.

It took many years of practice to become an accurate marksman. After honing my skill, I hit the center of targets at fifty paces, and with enough concentration, I was accurate enough to hit a target one hundred paces away. When I finally completed my training, I could extend my range to over two hundred paces away and became the most accomplished marksman in our class. Our teacher, Horace, had the craftsman make me an elite hunting bow as a reward for obtaining the highest skill. It has been at my side for over ten years and has served me well both on the hunt and in battle.

Can I take a closer look? It is a fine piece of artistry. What astounding detail. He had great skill; this is among the finest bows I have ever seen.

It is an excellent weapon, but you need more than a good weapon to be a skilled hunter or warrior. This brings me to the final part of my story. Once we reached the age of sixteen, our apprenticeship was complete. Two of my closest companions, Larce, and Tarsus, had become like brothers to me. During those years, we were rarely seen apart.

Upon completion, we were assigned to our village militia to separate companies. Only through Horace's influence could we stay together within the archery company.

We were sent out on a mission within that first month of joining the militia. We had received word that a small band of thieves had stolen cattle from one of our settlements to the west. We were charged with capturing them and recovering the stolen cattle. It wasn't long before we were on their trail. Moving cattle through the hill country will leave a noticeable trace, so they were easy to follow.

We spotted them within a two-day march and planned to ambush them right before they awoke. Just before dawn, we crept in close to them. We were able to awaken them with a dagger right to their necks. They surrendered without a fight. The punishment for stealing cattle was severe. It was up to the king to decide upon the exact sentence. If a criminal had been given the death penalty, they had the right to choose the method. Most choose the quickest and least painful, a knife to the throat. Caught red-handed stealing cattle, these men could be sentenced to death. The fear of this fate made them extremely dangerous. Later that evening, two of them tried to escape. One managed to loosen the wrappings of the other, and they quickly made a run for it into the night. Within minutes they were noticed missing, and our pursuit ensued. By daylight, we had picked up their trail. And by noon the next day, we had spotted them. Resisting or escaping is just caused for the use of deadly force to re-capture them. This is precisely what the commander had in mind. The order was given for them to be killed on sight. That was to be their fate now.

We approached when they paused to drink at a small stream hidden by tall grass. When we were within range, Larce, Tarsus, and I were given the order to pick a target and strike to kill. Tarsus and I shot, both hitting our mark. But Larce froze, unable to let his arrow fly. His target started heading for cover, running across the stream. I ran closer and took a second strike, and he went down. The commander was furious at Larce for not following his orders, and he was to be disciplined harshly upon returning to the village. Failure to follow a direct command was severe enough, but cowardness in battle was considered an even worse offense.

Once we returned, Larce was given his choice of punishment. Either be permanently expelled from the militia or accept a three-year exile with an offer to reenlist upon returning. Larce agreed to the three-year banishment. But we knew that no one had ever returned to the village following three years of exile. So, we were sure we would never see our friend again.

Before his sentence was enforced, Tarsus and I offered to serve a year of self-banishment towards Larce's sentence and lessen his time. Our request was brought straight to the king. His lordship, honoring the kinship among us, agreed. The exile of all three of us began three full moons ago, which now brings us up to our meeting.

Where are your friends now, Matteo?

As fate would demand, a violent storm erupted during a hunt soon after our first full moon. It went on for hours, and we became separated. The forest was devastated, tree after tree was uprooted, and low-lying areas were completely flooded. I searched for them for weeks, but it was impossible to find any signs of either Larce or Tarsus or retrace my steps back to our camp. Just over a month later, I came across Larce. He was dead, lying at the bottom of a raven with his leg badly broken. His hands and arms were covered with bite marks, sustained while fending off an attacking wolf. I buried him deep into the ground, and he now rests peacefully with the gods. To this day, I've not seen a trace of Tarsus. Our banishment ends in the spring, but I cannot bear to ever return to our village. I will never forget or forgive what has happened to my friends.

The mark of a wolf below your name on your bow. Why a "wolf"?

Well, that's my nickname, *Lupis*, the Wolf.

Why the wolf?

My friends say I would make a growling noise when pulling back my bowstring to strike. Larce was the first to call me that, and it just stuck. My teacher Horace had that bow maker Nerie add it to my bow.

Matteo, the wolf. Do you still growl like one while aiming your bow?

I'm not sure. I may. I'm only thinking of one thing while aiming to hit my mark.

Let's see. Take a strike at that white birch over there. Yes, I hear it. You do growl just like a wolf. You are *Matteo Fremitus Lupi* (Matteo, the growling wolf).

It was dawn before our conversation ended, but I was still too cautious about our newfound friend to allow myself much sleep. We had learned more about each other that night than most learned about a friend in a year. I knew from our conversation that this chance encounter in the woods would change our lives forever.

Blacksmith Shop, Village of Tressia

Well, done, my sons, a successful hunt, and you've returned with more ore. Toscano, how was Nico here? Was he helpful on the hunt?

He was, in many ways.

You both have already done some feasting on this roebuck, I see.

We did, along with a stranger we encountered on the hunt. We thought it wise to share the kill with him instead of fighting over it.

Yes, that was wise. Tell me more about this stranger.

We can, but we can do even better than that. Father, I want you to meet Matteo, our fellow hunter and recently found friend.

It is a pleasure to meet you, sir.

30

Well, this is unexpected. It is a pleasure to meet you, Matteo. You're full of surprises, Toscano. I must learn all about this encounter.

You will, tonight, father, but first, I need to introduce Matteo to his lordship.

Council Chambers of the Village of Tressia

It has been a pleasure meeting you, Matteo. If you don't mind, I need to discuss some personal business with Toscano for a few moments.

Certainly, your Lordship.

Toscano, join me in my chambers for a moment.

Yes, of course, my lord.

Toscano, this Matteo, where he's from, the village of Vacalvi, as you know, we have a good reason not to trust anyone from that city, including him. He may be concealing portions of his story and here with unknown intentions.

Like you, my lord, I did have reservations about him, but I also sensed his honesty and put belief in his words. He has had opportunities to harm us over these past few days, but he has not.

Remain cautious and watch him closely until
we are surer of him. Remember, Toscano,
this world is hostile, and deception is
rampant and often used to gain an advantage.

I will, my lord.

Home of Toscano

Nico, wake up. Father needs our help loading
his wagon. Come on, Nico, it's well past time
to get up. The harvest festival will be starting
soon.

Leave me be. It is still dark.

Now, Nico, get up. Father will be leaving
soon.

I know why you rush, my brother. You don't
want to miss a moment with your farm girl.

She is not just a farm girl.

Oh, that's right, she is your fair maiden farm
girl.

Now you sound a little jealous, my brother.
Your future fair maiden may be among those
arriving today with her. Don't you remember
her lovely young sister?

The Blacksmith Shop

Smithy, can you show me that lovely copper bowl, up there, on that corner shelf?

This one, my lady? Why, of course.

These details and artistry are exquisite.

Yes, the craftsman is very skilled.

Is it your work, Toscano?

No, no, it's my father. His talents are much sought after throughout the valley.

I can see why. And what are your talents, Toscano?

They are more with a bow and sword, my lady.

That sounds dangerous.

Oh, it is my lady, but my skill rivals his. Gia, the moon will be full tonight, and I have a special place I would like to show you after our meal.

What place is this, Toscano?

It is called the Cave of the Stars, just outside the village. It's beautiful on a clear night, especially with a full moon.

It sounds like a perfect place for a stroll after our meal.

The Cave of the Stars

This place is remarkable.

Here, sit, lay back. Now, look up. Look out just above the horizon, there. See those stars aligned in a square.

Where? I don't see it.

I'll trace them. Follow my finger.

Oh yes, I see it.

They say that is the window the gods passed through to reach us on their way to earth.

I can see why. It's all so beautiful.

It is, but it doesn't compare to the beauty I see when I look at you, Gia. I have thought about this moment with you. What it would be like for us to be alone. To have you next to me, holding you tight in my arms, your body next to mine.

And I've constantly thought about being with you, Toscano, and what I would feel when our lips touched, and our bodies held close together. I am never letting you go.

CHAPTER 4: THE RAIDERS

Tressia Military Barracks

Toscano, the sentry, has spotted smoke rising over the ridge line. He thinks it's Brescia.

Grab your weapon and find Matteo. I'll meet you at the stables. We must ride to Brescia at once.

Toscano, we're losing you. Toscano!

Matteo, search the village, see if anyone's alive. Nico, check the surrounding woods. I'll head down to the river.

Toscano, it's a massacre. There's no one left alive, only the bodies of butchered men and small children.

What about the women? Did you find any women? Are there any women?

No, there're no women here.

They've taken them. We must catch up to these butchers before dark.

Over here, Toscano, fresh wagon marks.

They're headed east.

Toscano, look up there, near the top of that hill.

I see them, and they carry captives.

Toscano, we are only three; they're ten, many more.

They have Gia and others. You can stay back if you wish, but I'm going after them.

I'm with you, Toscano.

So am I.

My brave brother and friend, our destiny is tied together forever. Let's move.

Matteo, do you have any idea where these raiders are from?

It is impossible to know at this distance.

It is possible, based on what I have seen before.

What do you mean?

Vacalvi, I have seen their raiding parties before. Matteo, you may know some of those we are about to kill.

These are not men I knew. It's the work of those who have turned cold and ruthless, murderers of innocents, raiding villages, and killing children. My destiny is to avenge these deaths, same as you.

You will, my friend.

Look, on that rise, how many do you see, Nico?

I count six, no, seven. There's one scouting ahead.

What do you think we should do, Toscano?

We stay close to them 'till dark. Once they make camp, we wait to see who goes on watch. Nico, you circle silently around them on the left. Matteo, you rotate slowly to the right. I'll give you both time to get into position. Go carefully, keeping low, getting close enough to take a clean shot, and wait for my signal. Stay ready with your bows drawn. I'll be moving into a position to take out that sentry. Listen to this. It's my birdcall. When you hear it, that's the signal to let your arrows strike. Then, charge the camp. No one is to be left standing. There's no mercy for what they have done. They all deserve to die. Are you both clear?

Yes.

Yes.

Nico, what's bothering you?

I've never struck down a man before, Toscano. I'm not sure I can do it. Not even to men like these.

Nico, we have no choice. They're murdering raiders. They butchered an entire village, slaughtering young children. They wouldn't hesitate a second to do it again, killing anyone they choose. It's up to us to stop them. This is our destiny. You can do this, Nico; we'll do it together. Remember your dawning when you drew up your courage for the first time? Feed on that feeling, my brother. It'll serve you well here.

It's time to move into position. As soon as you hear my call, we strike. We'll catch them off guard if we're lucky and finish them all quickly. Are you both ready?

Yes.

Yes. I'm ready.

May the will of the gods be done. Let's go.

Toscano, behind you, drop!

Well done, Matteo!

I couldn't let him get you away from buying me that round of wine you owe me.

And now, for stopping a blade from getting stuck in my back, I owe you another round, my friend.

Toscano, come, they're over here.

Gia! Thanks to the gods! You're alive!

Toscano!

Your shaking, Gia. It's over, Gia. I'm here. They're dead. Are you hurt?

It was so horrible, Toscano.

You're safe now, Gia. It's over.

Vera, are you hurt?

My father! My mother! The children! All of them, they killed them all, Toscano.

I know, I know. I am so sorry, Gia. Vera, I'm so sorry.

The village, everything, they burned everything! They hunted them down and killed them—everyone but us. My gods, my parents, my poor mother and father, they butchered them right in front of us, and my gods, the children! What are we going to do? Oh, my gods, my poor parents. Those poor children.

Gia, look at me. Hold me. You're safe now, Gia.

Toscano, my poor parents, killed them. Toscano, they're gone.

I know. They're paid for what they did. They're dead. They got what they deserved. We must leave this place now. There soon may be others. We must go now. Ride with me.

Nico, take their weapons and let's move. I want to be far away from here before the morning light.

The Village of Tressia

The village was close to panic when we returned. Hearing our news, most were expecting an attack at any moment. King Acri called for calm and sent emissaries to our surrounding villages, alerting them of the burning and butchery done at Brescia. He called for a meeting of the Council of Elders to unite the whole valley and stop these murderous invaders.

The Council Chambers were overflowing when I was called to enter. Elders representing Tarchina, Ronaldone, Gantolino, and La Sassi were present.

Toscano, come in. We're here to forge an alliance and to join our armies to defeat these invaders and rid our land of this killing and pillaging. Tell us, Toscano, what you have seen and done to a group of these raiders, and tell them what you believe we must do to stop them all.

My lords, the men we face are no ordinary farmers armed with pitchforks or even hunting bows for weapons. These are highly skilled, well-armed, trained warriors. They're here, driven desperate by disease and starvation, to raid and pillage our towns to survive.

The only way to stop them is to raise an army of our own and confront them. We need an army of warriors trained to fight like them. But it must be more forceful, better trained, and better equipped than the enemy we face. This is the only way we can defeat them. If we do not and are not prepared to fight as one, we will be slaughtered, conquered, and stripped of our land and lives.

What proof do you have about this enemy army and the danger you say we face?

My proof, Lord Altare, is in the faces of those we re-captured and with the bodies of those slaughtered, including children, lying dead in their burning village. And with these. Look at these swords and daggers. They were retrieved from the raiders we caught and ambushed. They were skillfully made and well-used. Look at the engraving on their heels, "Village of the Vacalvi." All their weapons carry this marking. Our lords, we are already at war. The enemy is already here. They will do whatever it takes to steal our food and destroy us. We have no time to waste; we must unite now to defeat them, or we all shall perish.

Well said, Commander. Now, it is time to decide. Let us hear from each one of you. Are we united and stand as one and defeat this enemy? First, let us hear from Ronaldone. Unitumi Vincimus?

Unitumi Vincimus!

Gantolino? Unitumi Vincimus?

Unitumi Vincimus!

La Sassi? Unitumi Vincimus?

Unitumi Vincimus!

And Tarchina? Unitumi Vincimus?

Unitumi Vincimus!

Council Chambers of King Acri

Toscano, now that the Council of Elders has agreed to unite our forces, it must have a commander. It must be one who can prepare our army for what is to come. Toscano, we all believe you are the most capable for this position. Will you stand with Tressia and our neighbors and accept the offer to command our military?

My lord, I am honored and humbled by your faith in me. I do accept this command and will serve with all my ability.

Congratulations Commander, we begin at once. How large of a force do you think we will need?

With the proper fortifications in the villages, at least two hundred strong, if they are well trained, armed, and ready to fight.

Two hundred men? That number of men will be challenging to recruit.

Who said they had to be just men, my lord? Some women are also willing to serve. But whomever we recruit, they will be useless unless they are armed and trained with proper weapons and will be quickly slaughtered against these well-trained and armed warriors. Most now barely have suitable bows and even fewer with swords or shields. Without these, we'll be slain. Our blacksmiths are already smelting ore, day and night, and cannot do more.

Toscano, you have my permission to recruit the blacksmiths needed, even construct a second furnace, and double the mining crew if necessary. Enlist the artisans required to produce the quality bows, shields, and armor you need. Report back to me on your progress. I want a two-hundred-strong fighting force fully armed, trained, and ready for battle by month-end.

Thank you, my lord, it will be done.

The Village of Tarchina

My Lord, may I speak freely?

You may Cintello; your most valuable advice arrives when you do so.

Thank you, my lord. I have reservations concerning this alliance, the joining our forces with that of the village of Tressia.

Continue, Cintello.

What do we know about this Toscano? What may be the true intentions of Tressia? Commanding an army of that size has never been done before, and it comes with imposing power. Toscano will control a large group of our men. If he fails and our men are lost, this entire valley will be left defenseless.

I see your point, Cintello. We must minimize the risk with this alliance. Include an agent of yours among the men we are sending to Tressia. Have him report to us anything he sees that could be endangering our rule or the safety of Tarchina.

It will be done as you wish, my Lord.

Militia Barracks, The Village of Tressia

Matteo, how goes the training of the La Sassi and Ronaldone recruits?

Commander, these men are farmers and a few skilled hunters, but they all have the will to fight to protect their homes. It will take time for them to obtain the skills we need, but they have the desire and know what's at stake.

Good, and how about the men of the Gantolini village?

We had an interesting start, but we understood each other much better once they realized I could cut open their throats before they could reach their swords. It will take time with them, but I will also make decent warriors of them.

And what of the men from Tarchina?

A mixed bag, Commander; there is underlying mistrust of our intentions with these men.

Who is leading this mistrust, Matteo?

It is this man named Silvius, Commander.

I want to get to know his face. Point him out to me on the march tomorrow. We must be formed into a cohesive fighting unit and have the trust of all our men if we succeed in battle. Watch him closely. If there are still questions surrounding this Silvius after tomorrow, we shall remove him and those aligned with him before this mistrust infects others. Tarchina has always been more of a rival than a good neighbor. That attitude must not be present on the battlefield; having all committed to our cause is vital.

Understood, Commander.

Tomorrow, for the first time, we march together as one. We will see if all our training can be implemented and learn how much

45

work is left to be done. Go now, the both of you, and get some rest. Tomorrow will be a challenging day.

We formed at daylight, ready to begin our first organized military exercise, a wargame simulation. Matteo had a wealth of military knowledge. His years of experience made him a valuable, innovative second in command. The combat training and tactics he had acquired were quickly put into practice. The advancement of our raw troops into a competent fight force over these last months was rapid and primarily due to him.

For this exercise, the men were divided into four companies consisting of ten to twelve men, two infantry companies, one archery, and one cavalry company. Each was trained explicitly on what was expected during these unified maneuvers, and we now had the beginnings of an organized tactical fighting force.

The Lemon Forest

The men were anxious to put their month of training to the test. The war games started by separating our army into two groups, attacking the other in a mock ambush. The first group I placed under the command of Matteo. He was to continue advancing along the river while the second group, under my control, remained along the bank of the Fiora, giving them a 2-hour head start.

Matteo was to ambush us at a time and place that encompassed a strategic advantage and the elements of surprise.

No one was to be injured. All weapons were placed in the supply wagon. The combat was to be close, hand to hand, using mock weapons. The losers were the combatants who were forced to the ground.

The tension dramatically increased once we separated. I desired to evaluate our strategies and tactics and instill leadership skills, comradery, and discipline into the men. Using a wargame exercise is the best way to accomplish these.

The timing and location of the ambush were perfect. The attack immediately boxed us in. Matteo used his reserves brilliantly, bringing them into battle at the right time. They successfully divided and overwhelmed our smaller, vulnerable groups as the opportunity arose. It was surprising how quickly his maneuvering overcame us.

The men witnessed first-hand how effective a coordinated and well-executed tactical maneuver can be.

My group was getting routed, and I ordered them to fall back and reform strategically. Discipline made the difference in holding us together as we retreated and reformed. We began to rally, turning more into a brawl than a strategic exercise, so I ordered all to stand down and ended the training exercise.

After bandaging up some cuts, and one badly busted fist, we begin our march back to Tressia.

The men got their first real taste of fighting in organized combat and benefited from a morale boost.

We started our march back to Tressia, walking in a file, two by two, following the bank of the Fiora River. Before we advanced our first mile, I heard the clashing of shields and swords rising from the rear of the formation. Within seconds we were under a barrage of arrows and javelins, many hitting their mark.

I heard from the distance Matteo giving the order to form a shield wall across his rear line and for his archers to form up behind them. This quick thinking bought us some time. I ordered the men to me to close ranks and prepare for a full-on charge that was sure to come. It did, and it was brutal.

We were attacked, battling ferociously on all three sides, with our backs to the Fiora River. Matteo's rear shield wall collapsed, and his men began to race toward us, hoping to save their lives. We fought bravely, but we were outnumbered, and many were overmatched, falling to their death by the fierce assault of wheeling battle axes and crushing blows of heavy swords. We were facing total annihilation. Then, on the opposing riverbank of the river, I saw a chance for our last desperate attempt to survive and ordered the army to retreat across the river to higher ground. We formed a new defensive line to make a final stand there. Through the grace of the gods, the river at this point had narrowed and rose only to hip depth. Those who endured the onslaught waded across the river, dragging the wounded and their weapons. Once on the other side, the men gathered, locking their shields and ready for a final assault. The enemy seeing this, paused for a moment, unsure about continuing. This pause gave us confidence and the time to set our defenses fully. I ordered our archers to move to the front line and begin firing straight into the enemy. As the gods allowed, we struck down several, including their commander. Stunned and confused, they turned and began to retreat.

The men gave out a defiant yell, knowing that they had just succeeded in fending off the attack and would survive.

The battle may have been over, but we were far from safety. Our march back to Tressia could still be a dangerous one. Thanks to the gods, rewarding us for our courage, we did not meet the enemy on our return.

We were brutally battered but not defeated. Our losses were painful, with twenty-two men dead and fifteen wounded, three of them severely. I estimated that we inflicted half of those losses upon the enemy. Upon returning to the village, I ordered our remaining archers to the walls to prepare for an attack.

We had survived, rallying with our courage. What was supposed to be a bloodless wargame exercise had turned into the battle of our lives.

CHAPTER 5: THE SPECULATORS

Council Chambers of King Acri

Toscano, you were caught entirely by surprise, unaware of the enemy's location and strength. You were only saved from total disaster by your quick thinking and the skill and bravery of you and your men.

That is true, my lord. I will abide by your wishes if you wish to release me from my command.

No, that is not what I am considering. I have faith in you, Toscano. You have learned a valuable lesson that will serve us well in the future.

What are you suggesting, my lord?

I do not wish our army ever to be caught in a comparable situation. We must know what threats we face. To that end, I would like for you to form a specialized unit that can give us the information we need to be best prepared for battle composed of explorators and speculators. The explorators will be our mounted scouts. They will gather information on the terrain ahead of our army, locating them and estimating their strength. They will identify the hazards and specify the ideal high ground to set your line of attack and the location of your camp. With this knowledge, you will make informed decisions placing your army in the best possible position.

Incredibly wise, my lord.

These speculators will function as your spies, gathering information behind the enemy lines and enlisting collaborators to infiltrate enemy cities. They are to seek strategic information on our enemies and inform you of the things before they happen.

I can see how all this will be valuable, my lord. I will start right away and find the right men for this unit.

The speculator's position, Toscano, is the most dangerous and requires deep deceptions. Please consider both men and women for this position. Women can have potent methods of persuasion over unsuspecting men that can be quite effective in producing the information we seek.

True, my lord. It will be done.

Tressia Tavern

Matteo, let's take a walk outside. I want to ask you something and don't want to be overheard.

Certainly, Commander.

Matteo, tell me more about Vacalvi and who comes and goes freely into the city.

As with any city of its size, many enter and leave daily. Plenty of merchants looked to sell their wine, pottery, tools, weapons, and armor. Then the mystics, healers, and minstrels make their rounds into the city. For the ladies, there are also jewelry merchants selling all kinds of brooches, necklaces, and bracelets, crafted in silver and gold, obsidian, and seashells from as far away as Sicily and Greece. But about this time, many more farmers enter with their wagons full of produce, herders looking to sell pigs and cattle during harvest season.

It sounds like it would be a busy gate.

Yes, there are days you must push to enter.

And are all these traders known to the guards? Or are those unfamiliar also entering freely into the city?

Most of them are familiar, but a few merchants traveling from afar would be new to the city; they enter right along.

Good, thank you, Matteo. This is helpful. Now, please go back inside. I will join you a bit later.

Militia Barracks

Nico, the king, wishes to learn about Vacalvi from a source inside the city, especially about their military strength and movements, anything that would aid us in a battle that is surely coming. I have a way we can get this information using that merchant, Cristo. He was here late yesterday and could not have gotten far. At first light, could you find him? Let him know you are on orders of the king. Tell him the queen would like to see him and buy some jewelry for the festival. Bring him straight to me. Tell him I need to speak with him first.

It will be done, Commander.

Well, Cristo, thank you for returning.

My pleasure, Commander. I have some exceptional pieces that I know the Queen will enjoy.

Cristo, I brought you back here to talk to you about more than your visit with the queen.

You have?

Yes, the king has something more he would like you to do for him. It is something you will be paid for very handsomely.

I'm listening, Commander.

He needs your stop next to Vacalvi.

But I left there not long ago, and I am now heading south, Commander.

Not anymore. You will be heading back to Vacalvi.

Why there, Commander?

We are concerned about what is happening there, and you have the perfect cover to get us more information.

But I am just a traveling jewelry merchant, not a spy.

Exactly, a diligent, well-traveled jewelry merchant who has a good memory. I am sure you hear and talk to many customers on your visits, moving from tavern to tavern, street to street, market to market. You must meet and speak with many villagers, tradespeople, other merchants, wealthy nobles, and lords.

Of course, that's the work of my trade. I meet and deal with many, with some talking to no end. At times it isn't easy to close the sale.

Good, that's why you're our ideal contact there. You need to listen carefully and relay what you've learned to us.

So, you do want me to be a spy?

Don't be alarmed. You'll not be doing anything different from what you are doing now. All I am asking of you now is to listen closely to what you are being told. And remember all the details. The better you relay information to us, the greater your reward.

It sounds dangerous, and I am incredibly leery of this work.

Cristo, I'm not asking you to become a full-time spy. You are to remain, Cristo, the jewelry merchant. Only now are you to use your good memory and listening skills.

Let's say I agree to become this spying messenger for you. How rich of a reward are you considering?

What is your profit on a good day of selling?

Fifteen coins on a good day, and I have made twenty after visiting the queen.

You will have your visit today with the queen, plus you will be paid fifty coins upon relaying the information from Vacalvi upon your return. Cristo, by helping us, you will also have the gratitude of our king. That is worth more than any coin.

Tell me, Commander, what kind of information will I relay to you if I agree?

It will be information that will help us learn about their army's military strength and movements. Knowing this in advance is the most valuable information we could have. We will be relying on you to remember all you are told carefully.

Who are you planning for me to contact in Vacalvi, and how will I know this person?

I have devised an exchange so you will quickly identify him. What is your most prized jewelry piece?

It's my granulated gold brooch set with a blue sapphire gemstone surrounded by a ring of red rubies.

Good, you will be contacted in the market by someone looking for a unique gift for his lover, Letitia. He will mention her name and that she favors a brooch. You are to make a trade with him with your prized jewelry piece. You can trust he is with us. Listen to him carefully. Once your sale is complete, leave at once and return directly here.

I am very apprehensive about all of this, Commander.

Cristo, all you need to do is listen. You will be doing his lordship a great honor he will not soon forget.

It sounds too dangerous for me.

Cristo, I'm not asking you to do much more than you usually do. You are just a typical, friendly merchant hoping to make a sale; it's not complicated. When you arrive in Vacalvi, you are to function as expected. Stay until a particular customer contact you and listen to what he tells you. That's it, Cristo, and you will be richly rewarded.

If I agree, it will be for this one time. I am hardly brave and have no desire to be a full-time spy.

As you wish.

How soon do you want me to start?

You are to leave for Vacalvi at dawn.

Council Chambers of the King Acri

My lord, we are here as you requested.

Yes, please come in. We have urgent matters to discuss. Matteo, Toscano speaks highly of you, and your skill and bravery have proven outstanding. He has also informed me more about the fate of your friends following your banishment from Vacalvi.

Yes, my Lord. Vacalvi was my home, but no longer. I serve you and Tressia now.

That is good to hear, Matteo, because I have something I need you to do, and it is something that only a man with your background can accomplish.

I am most willing, my Lord,

You should hear what I am asking you before you agree. This request will be most perilous.

58

I am listening, my Lord.

As you know, we face a formidable enemy in Vacalvi. We are still outmatched in strength and weaponry, even with our joint forces. We need an advantage if we are to even the coming fight. We need to know what we are facing and when. We need someone inside the city who is trusted and can freely gather this information. Matteo, you are that someone.

M Lord, you want me to return to Vacalvi and spy on them?

Yes, Matteo, I do, for a time. You are the best one to gather the information we need. Tressia will have a much greater chance to survive the coming war with your help Matteo. Are you willing? Are you ready to help us and become our unsuspecting spy in Vacalvi?

My Lord, I am.

Thank you, Matteo. The fate of Tressia lies in the success of this mission. Matteo, I know you are angry about the banishment of your close friend Larce and his death and that of your friend, Tarsus. This anger serves you well, but it cannot be seen in Vacalvi. You must be accepted back, unsuspectingly, in Vacalvi. You must push that anger down deep inside you and adopt the frame of mind you had when you were young and innocent. Can you do this, Matteo? Can you act like your loyalty still is with Vacalvi and earn their

trust so you can relay the information we
seek back to us?

I can and will, my Lord. I will do what needs
to be done.

I trust you will, Matteo. May the gods be with
you.

Etruria Circa 400 BC

CHAPTER 6: THE CITY OF VACALVI

The Gates of Vacalvi

Titus, come up here. You'll not believe who is approaching the city. Someone you might remember, look.

Can that be? By the grace of the gods, it's Matteo.

Matteo, you're alive.

Very much so, Titus.

We all thought you were dead. It is good to see you again, my friend.

It is good to be alive and back here in the city.

Where are Tarsus and Larce? Are they not with you?

No, we were all separated in a violent storm months ago. I was hoping Tarsus returned here ahead of me. Larce is dead and killed from a fall into a ravine.

Come, let us bring the news of your return to the Commander. He will be pleased to see you again.

What of my family, my mother and my father? And Janus?

Matteo, as you can see, we are in a harsh famine, and disease has spread throughout the city. Many are sick, and many more have already died. Your father was among the first, and then your mother. Your brother, Janus, praise to the gods, is alive. In your father's footsteps, he serves us well as the finest leather smith in Vacalvi. Matteo, where are you going?

Home of Matteo and Janus

Matteo, thank the gods, you're alive! I'm so happy to see you.

As I am you, my brother.

So much has happened since you have gone. Mother and father, Matteo, they are gone, both gone.

I know, Janus. I should never have left. I'm so sorry.

It's not your fault. It is this place. First, the farmers got sick, with whole families perished. Then the crops were abandoned in the fields. With little food, the people in the city started to starve, and soon disease took hold of the city. It spread so quickly that many died within days. First in their homes and soon right in the markets and streets. There were so many bodies that they were where they dropped. People began to flee, abandoning the city in waves. Father wanted us to go too, but mother insisted it would be too dangerous and wanted to be here for your return. She was afraid that we would be attacked on the road. What little food we had would have certainly been stolen. Soon father fell ill. Mother tended to him day and night, right to the end, but there was little she could do to save him. Days later, she fell ill. Matteo, it was dreadful. She died in my arms, telling me not to be sad. She was joining our father in the spirit world. She told me you would return and that we would again be close, as close as we were as boys.

She was right, Janus. We are together. And I know we'll get through this if we stay together.

She left this package for you and told me to keep it safe until you return.

My Ballista! I've forgotten all about it and my training bow. I'm happy you kept these for me.

The Barracks of Vacalvi

Welcome back, Matteo. Most assumed you would never return. But I had faith you'd be back. It is good to see you again, Matteo.

Thank you for that faith, Commander. And now that I am back, how may I serve you again?

Matteo, as you can see, we are in very troubling times. Many are starving and suffering from sickness. We need courageous leaders like yourself, now more than ever. You have always been among our most ambitious, so I'm appointing you a company commander. You deserve it, Matteo. You have proven your loyalty by returning here to the city. You already know most of the men, but our mission has changed. We are not here to defend the city. Our mission is to secure enough food to feed the entire city.

Have we become raiders?

It is sad to think so, but famine, death, and disease have killed or driven away hundreds from the city. To endure, we must secure enough food for the city until the new harvest.

So, we ambush, kill, and take what we need.

Matteo, it is not pleasant work, I know, but without it, there would be no Vacalvi. Can I count on you, Matteo?

Commander, Vacalvi is a far different place from the one I left. Both my parents are gone. Many of the people I have known are dead, sick, or starving; this is my home. I'll do what needs to be done.

I knew I could count on you, Matteo. These past few months, we have been raiding throughout the valley. And now, many of the closest farms have been stripped clean. So, we must go out further south to get what we need. We are going as far south as Tressia to bring back all the crops and livestock we can carry.

I understand, Commander.

Good. I'm glad to have you back, Matteo.

Vacalvi Market

Most now are looking for food or weapons, my friend, and you are looking for a gift?

Yes, a special gift, a brooch, for my love, Letitia. We are to be married.

Oh, I see. I believe I do have a special gift that will fit your purpose. Right here, a gold brooch. It is set with a bright blue sapphire, surrounded by a ring of rubies. How does that sound?

It sounds lovely.

Here it is.

It is lovely. How much is it? Let me pay you.

Your words are payment enough, my friend.
What do you have to tell me?

The city is in the grip of famine, struck by
disease and death. Hundreds have already
died or fled.

Yes, that is quite clear.

The city is desperate for food, barely enough
to survive the coming winter. It is on the
verge of total collapse. The king has pressed
the army into becoming full-time raiders to
seize enough food to feed the remaining
population. It's a force of over two hundred
in mounted cavalry. It's been ordered to
scour the land farther south, heading toward
Tressia. They leave in two days.

Very distressing news. How do you know all
of this, my friend?

Because it is I, who will lead them.

**The Village of Tressia, Council Chambers
of the King Acri**

My lord, I have news from Vacalvi.

Go ahead, Toscano, I am most interested to
hear.

The city is on the verge of collapse; disease
and famine have gripped the city. Hundreds
are already dead, and many more hundreds
have been driven away. They are growing

66

more desperate for food and have ordered their entire army to become raiders. Their cavalry, of over two hundred strong, is about to leave the city and head our way.

Excellent work, Toscano. Our surrounding villages will be a tempting target. I will call for the harvest to begin now. All their crops and livestock will be brought into the city at once.

I will double the number of our scouts and patrols. We will be ready, my lord.

There is one more thing we must do.

Home of Matteo and Janus

Janus, the army, leaves at dawn. We head over from the highland to the valley south in search of food for the city. You must join us. Grab what you can carry. We leave at dawn.

Matteo, I am no warrior. I must stay here and wait for your return.

Janus, trust me, this city is on the verge of collapse, and this is the only way I can protect you. You must come with me, and I have the plan to save us both.

And leave this place now, we will have nothing?

Janus, there is more to my banishment than I have told. You must trust me and come with me before it is too late.

The Lemon Forest

Commander, our scouts reported a large group of skirmishers two hours ahead, heading towards the Fortress Rofalco.

We keep moving until we find a suitable camp a mile from the fortress.

Fortress Rofalco

Commander, the Fortress Rofalco is all clear.

Good, we set camp inside the fortress for the night.

Janus, wake up. We must go. I have someone I would like you to meet.

Who? Where are we going?

Come on, get up and follow me. It's not far.

Commander, Nico, it is good to see you two again.

Matteo, I trust all went well. Indeed, I travel with the entire army of Vacalvi.

Excellent, and who is this you bring to meet us?

This is my brother Janus. Janus, this is Toscano and his brother Nico. These are the friends I met close to this very spot during my exile.

It's a pleasure to meet you both finally. Matteo speaks very highly of both of you.

We feel the same and more about him.

I remember that evening well, Matteo. We spoke the entire night and almost ate a whole roebuck.

Nico, you certainly have a talent for roasting roebuck, and I've never eaten as well since.

That evening, we learned much about you and your youth growing up in Vacalvi.

Matteo, can we speak privately for a moment?

Yes, Commander.

The Vacalvian Camp at Fortress Rafalco

Men gather around. I have someone with me who would like to speak with you. Gather around. He's a friend I met some time ago, near this very spot, during my exile. He's the

Tressian commander. Please listen carefully to what the Commander has to say. Commander.

Men of Vacalvi, my name is Toscano, and I am here to speak with you under a flag of truce. Matteo and I are indeed friends and have been for a long while. I have learned much from him and recently learned about your city's condition. I'm saddened to hear what is happening there and the suffering of your people. Men, you are warriors, proud warriors of Vacalvi. You have fought bravely, with honor, defending your once great city. But now, you honor a failing city on the verge of collapse. It has become so desperate that your king commands you to do cruel and dreadful acts to survive. He's ordering this once noble army to attack and kill defenseless civilians, men, women, and children, stealing their food in a blatant attempt to feed his starving population. You have been reduced from a once-proud army to a gang of murdering raiders. My fellow warriors, it is too late for Vacalvi. It has been too severely struck by disease, death, and famine to hold on any longer.

I can offer you a way to save yourselves and your families. By my king's declaration, I can give you a chance to start a new life, a new life in Tressia, an opportunity to serve a vibrant city and a new King. Join us, renounce your loyalty to Vacalvi and live a proud military life once again as citizens in the army of Tressia. Those with family in Vacalvi will be given a chance to retrieve them and return to Tressia. The choice is yours, remain loyal to a dying city and a cruel king, or join us and become true warriors again and lead an honorable life. You and your families will be welcomed in Tressia and allowed to begin a new life and be proud warriors again.

Men, the commander, speaks the truth. He's a man of his word and carries the faith of his king. He has proven that he's a man who can be trusted. His king is also fair and wise, and Tressia has become prosperous. It will welcome all of you as it has me. You are free to choose, remain loyal to Vacalvi, a city on the threshold of collapse, or join me now and pledge your loyalty to Tressia. When word spreads that there will be no food coming from this raiding, utter panic in the city will surely erupt and spell the end of Vacalvi. It would be wise to quickly gather your family and what belongings you can carry and head here when this happens. Now is the time you need to decide. Men, are you ready to start anew? Join us, and your families will be safe.

Council Chambers of King Acri

Well done, you have not only thwarted the attack from Vacalvi but have completely neutralized an enemy. How many have renounced Vacalvi and pledged loyalty to us?

Most have pledged allegiance to you and asked to be welcomed to Tressia. There are

72

Twenty returning to Vacalvi to be reunited with their families. But many of those are planning to travel back here with them.

Toscano, you and a company of your men will go to Vacalvi along with ambassador Titus. He will deliver our truce offer to King Darius and relay his response to me. Any of those wishing to leave Vacalvi, you will escort them back here.

Council Chambers of King Darius of Vacalvi

Welcome, Ambassador; what news do you bring me from the great city of Tressia?

I bring you the news that little is left of your once great army.

What are you saying?

What little of your army remains in a Tressian camp outside the city.

You are lying. My men are loyal to me.

Many of your men have renounced you, King Darius, and pledged loyalty to Tressia and my king.

No, this cannot be true. My army will be returning with wagons full of supplies any day now, as they have before.

Not this time, your lordship. Your army is no more, and I offer you a truce and supplies if you pledge to end your raiding in our valley.

Guards, take this man away and cast him out of the city. I will hear no more of these lies from him. Bring my counselor to me at once!

Tressian Camp on the outskirts of Vacalvi

Commander, come, you must see this. It's Ambassador Titus, and he is leading what's left in the city and is heading this way.

It looks as though we will have plenty of company on our way back to Tressia. Advance the cavalry. There is no telling what King Darius might do when he realizes those remaining in his once-proud city are abandoning him.

Council Chambers of King Darius

My lord, there's a mass exodus from the city, and the Tressian cavalry is escorting them.

Let them go. We'll have fewer mouths to feed. Open the stores for those who have remained. Loyalty is to be rewarded.

Council Chambers of King Altare of Tarchina

My Lord, we are receiving reports of a mass exodus from Vacalvi, and the city is being abandoned.

Bring me my fastest scout. I have a message for him to bring to King Darius.

Council Chambers of King Darius of Vacalvi

King Darius, I am aware of your current hardship. If conditions force you to leave Vacalvi, I can offer you a haven here in Tarchina. It is a satisfactory settlement of significant acreage, producing abundant crops, and is available to you for a fair price. Our close alliance will hold great promise for both of us.

My messenger can be entrusted to secure your reply,

King Altare of Tarchina

Messenger, here is my reply. Take it with urgent speed back to your King.

75

Village of Tressia

Commander, I have pressing news, the militia of Tarchina has left during the night.

All of them?

All, I'm afraid, persuaded no doubt by their leader Silvius.

I will speak to the King at once.

Chambers of King Acri

Trust and loyalty are not virtues honored in Tarchina.

There is more, your majesty. Our scouts have reported that King Darius and his entourage have departed Vacalvi with wagons full of supplies.

Where is he headed?

It is impossible to be sure at this point, but it's in the direction of Tarchina.

Commander, have our friendly jewelry merchant, Cristo, head out to Tarchina. We need to find out more about this potential alliance.

The City of Tarchina

Welcome, King Darius. I trust your journey was a safe one.

If you are wondering about the security of your payment, King Altare, the treasury of Vacalvi, has arrived intact with me.

Well, that is good news for both of us. Your new home awaits your arrival, and I'm sure you and your people will be pleased. But for now, you're my honored guest for this evening, and we have much to discuss.

Tell me more of what you know about my missing army.

I am afraid it is not good news, Darius. Your army is no more, and they have pledged allegiance to King Arci and their adopted city of Tressia. The Tressia commander arranged it, encouraged by your commander Matteo.

Matteo? My commander, Matteo?

Yes, you were deceived by him, Darius. Our contacts within Tressia confirmed that he was not what he seemed to be upon returning from exile.

That traitor, he will pay for what he has done to me.

Well, it is good that you are here then, and I can aid you in getting your revenge.

CHAPTER 8: FANUM VOLTUMNAE

People throughout Etruria gathered at the Temple of Voltumnae for this year's vernal equinox celebration. The temple stood on a central plateau within sight of the city of Volsinii. The entrance was lined with gleaming white, towering marble columns. It had a deep orange terracotta roof adorned, on all sides, with statues of the lesser gods. It sat on a massive foundation, requiring climbing thirty steps to reach the entrance doorway. The interior was vast, with pillars running down each side. The space culminated with an enormous domed sanctuary. Elders from every league city crowded inside, crammed between the towering pillars. Many began to push forward to gain a front-row view of the upcoming proceedings. The Temple's entrance was perfectly aligned to catch the first rays of the vernal equinox yearly sunrise.

The excitement heightened as the sunlight began to stream into the temple. Rays of light extended across the temple floor and illuminated the massive rear altar. Within seconds, the space was bathed in bright sunshine. Above the crowd's clamor, you could hear the faint melody of flutes and a choir singing as a procession approached the temple. The assembly was gradually hushed as it entered.

The musicians entered first. Rows of them, marching in pairs, in dark green linen tunics, trimmed with bands of gold or red, over a white calf-length dress and high laced boots. They wore broad-brimmed felt petasos, the men in brown and the women capped in dark red with a higher crown. They played flutes and lyres as they marched forward. The music sounded mystical, almost hypnotizing the congregation. They were followed by the choir, rows of women dressed in flowing white gowns, snitched at the waist, and trimmed with a gold border ringing the bottom. Their costume was finished with a deep red cape draped gracefully from their shoulders.

Next, the apprentices swung censers of burning incense and perfume suspended from chains. The fragrances soon filled the entire temple. The priests and priestesses came next, donning high white, semi-conical hats trimmed in gold and wearing long white belted tunics over a white toga, each designated with a colored sash running across their chests, distinguishing their specific roles. The haruspices, entrusted with interpreting the entrails of animals, wore red sashes. Next were the augurs, bearing gold sashes, charged with interpreting the flights of birds and bolts of lightning and the sound of thunder to determine the gods' wishes.

The procession concluded with the High Priest, Jovan. He wore a blood-red hooded robe draped completely over his crowned head and tied with a thick white belt at the waist. He carried a long, curved staff tipped in gold, advancing slowly down the center aisle.

As the procession approached the altar, they separated, lines moving to either side. The music ended as the High Priest moved behind the raised stone slab altar. It was set directly in front of a towering bronze statue of the goddess Voltumnae. Her left arm raised to the heavens, grasping a flaming torch, illuminating the dome ceiling above her. Jovan turned and faced his congregation, slowly raising his arms to the sky, signaling the choir to again erupted in song. It was now time for the ritual sacrifices to begin. Those nearest the altar rushed forward, hoping for an unobstructed view of the ceremonies.

The bloodletting rituals went on for hours, with the different priests and priestesses analyzing the entails to interpret the will of the many gods. The ceremonies concluded with the anointing of the new priest and priestesses, followed by an even more majestic departing procession. As it started to descend the steps exiting the temple, I spotted Vera. I could barely recognize her as she was fully immersed in her new persona.

It was now time for the elders to convene their conference. It occurred in a majestic amphitheater on a hillside just north of the temple. The seats were carved right into the tuff stone, forming a circular-shaped terrace cut into the hillside. Every seat faced the marble podium that overlooked the picturesque expanse of the valley spreading out below it.

King Acri represented Tressia, accompanied by a group of eight wealthy nobles who joined him on this year's journey. It was King Arci's turn to officiate this year over the proceedings. Tensions were high, and the League of Twelve was shocked by the news of the total collapse of Vacalvi. King Arci's calming oratory helped to restore some stability. The debate now centered around the need for the cities to unify and respond when a member city faced an imminent attack or an internal collapse. It dragged on for hours. But no firm resolution could be reached.

King Acri hosted the League of Twelve at our encampment that evening at a delicious banquet. We were located on the edge of an enormous open field, a short walk from the Temple. Matteo and I were charged with securing the site. Our campsite was impressive, only surpassed by the host city, Volsinii. Six large tents were erected, enough to supply lodging for all in our party and shelter for the stores of supplies we carried to maintain us for the duration of the expedition. Like ours, many campsites were positioned close to the tree line, creating a small, close-knit village overnight. The feasting went well into the night, and I noticed that King Altare of Tarchina was the only one who left the festivities early.

It was just noon the next day before King Acri was ready to head out to the fairgrounds. They were already bustling with activity by the time we arrived.

For many, the start of sporting contests was the festival's highlight. The events took place in a gigantic stadium. It was the largest wooden structure I had ever seen, constructed by King Erucia of Volsinii. It could hold up to two thousand spectators. Outside the stadium were scores of merchants and craftsmen housed in rows of tent stalls. They offered everything you could imagine, from finely made copper, silver, and gold jewelry to exquisite bronze medallions, mirrors, and statues. Artisans could be seen working in metal, leather, wood, wool, and linen, producing many weapons, armaments, tools, utensils, pottery, textiles, and footwear. I couldn't help but purchase a stunning necklace for Gia.

And, of course, there was plenty of food and drink. I have never seen that much wine and food in one place before. Tents were filled with dozens of barrels of all shapes and sizes holding grain and producing in abundance, from barley, lentils, chickpeas, beans, cherries, lemons, oranges, and dates.

The aroma from the cooking fires was enticing as it drifted gently among the rows of stalls. The smells of roasted beef, rabbit, deer to wild boar were everywhere. When we neared one of the taverns, the King handed me some coins to go ahead and clear some tables so we could sit together and begin to feast.

My friends, his majesty, would like to buy you wine, but not just a cup here, a complete amphora.

To what do we owe this honor?

Here, take these coins, and you could ask him yourself on your way out.

Thank you, your majesty. We'll drink in your honor.

They seem happy enough.

Yes, my lord, quite happy, and they have an abundance of coins to keep them that way.

It was mid-afternoon by the time we made our way to the stadium. We were seated with the other royals in the reserved area, shaded from the intense afternoon sun. The athletes came from every city in the League, some as far away as Campania, fifty miles south. The wrestling and box matches were the main attractions for the first days. They were my favorite. The betting on them was frantic, with the winners pocketing a small fortune. The gladiator combats were a featured festival event and were saved for the final days. The most famous gladiator at this year's festival was Turcius of Alilia. He was a long-running, fast, and powerful champion with an enormous following. In his second bout, he was matched against a gladiator named Mancius of Tarchina. It looked like Turcius would be dethroned, and the betting became frantic. But with a furious finishing combination of blows, he was again victorious.

On the afternoon of day ten, it was time for the chariot races. As expected, they drew the largest crowds. There were scores of collisions and spectacular crashes, some causing brutal injuries and death. The crowd loved it. By the time of the final champion race, the excitement was fanatic. The noise level of the cheering crowd was almost deafening. This year's games were again a spectacular success. As the stadium emptied, the winds erupted ahead of a line of thick black clouds fast approaching. We quickly dashed back to our campsite but were soaked from head to toe. When we arrived, we found it fully packed and set to begin our journey back to Tressia.

CHAPTER 9: THE STAGE IS SET

Vera had moved seamlessly into her position as Alfia, the High Priestess of Tarchina. Her prophecies were shrewd when approached by the king, and she soon became well-respected by the entire court. It wasn't long before King Altare consulted her advice before every move. The stage was now set for our plan to start to produce results.

Court of King Altare

My lordship, our forces are now prepared to march on Tressia.

Good, keep them ready, Cintello, and wait for my orders.

The Temple of Menrva

What do you see, priestess? Does the goddess give us good fortune in our war with Tressia?

My lord, I foresee a great victory for you, but now is not the time. You must wait. The goddess is not ready to bestow her blessing, and it must occur at a time of her choosing, or you will fail, and Tarchina will pay a harsh price.

How much longer? When will it be time?

Soon, my lord, very soon.

The Marketplace of Tarchina

Good morning, Cristo.

Good morning to you, priestess. What may I show you this morning?

I am looking for a gift, a small dagger, perhaps?

A dagger?

Yes, it is for a close friend, and I would like to give it to him soon.

How soon? I can engrave it for you.

There is little time for that.

I see. How is this one, my priestess?

Yes, this will do very nicely.

Will there be anything else, priestess? I could stay a bit longer.

Oh no, you should leave. This gift is all. Where will you be heading next? Tressia, I presume.

Yes, my priestess. I'll be heading to Tressia once I leave here.

Well, it is a long journey, you should leave at once.

Yes, I will, thank you, priestess. And you, priestess, are you to be traveling soon?

Oh yes, very soon, I'll be traveling to Vipsul for my yearly retreat.

Well, may the gods bless us both on our journeys?

I will be praying to make it so.

Chambers of King Acri

My lord, Cristo, has brought news from Tarchina.

What has he learned, Commander?

She has asked for the dagger, my lord.

How soon?

Very soon, my lord, she told him he should leave at once.

And what of her?

She is also leaving and heading to Vipsul for her retreat to the school of Augurs there.

Good, follow the plan and get her back to Tressia.

Yes, my lord.

Toscano, I want to know when the
Tarchinian army leaves the city.

Yes, my lord. Our scouts are within sight of
the city as we speak.

Commander, are your men ready for battle?
It will soon be time to deal with our enemy
for the last time.

They are my lord. They're ready with their
lives.

The Temple of Menvra

My lord, come in. The goddess Tinia has
spoken, the heavens have revealed her
desires, and she has given her blessings. Your
destiny awaits. Go forth now and do what
you must. The time is now upon you.

Is victory certain?

Victory favors those brave enough to seize it,
now go, my lord, and do battle.

Chambers of King Altare

My lord, our high priestess has sent word
asking for your permission to leave for her
retreat to Vipsul.

I wish her safe travels, and she is to be escorted closely by our most trusted guards.

Yes, my Lord.

Oh, Cintello, she is not to leave their sight.

I understand, my lord.

Gia, we have heard from Vera.

How is she? Is she all right? I have been so worried.

She is safe. She has gained the trust of King Altare and was readily accepted by the court as their high priestess. She is remarkable and already on her journey out of the city.

She must come back here safely to us, or I will never forgive myself for letting her go.

Soon, Gia, soon. Nico is meeting her in Vipsul and bringing her back home.

Praise the gods, and we will have a huge feast to celebrate her return.

The gardens of the Temple of Aplu, the city of Vipsul

Vera, Vera, over here. Come closer.

Nico? Is that you?

Come closer but turn your back towards me and continue your prayers. Your guards from

Tarchina watch your every move, and they must not see you speaking with me.

I understand.

Listen carefully. We have the plan to get you safely back to Tressia. Your work is done in Tarchina, and it Is far too dangerous for you to be there any longer.

I am listening.

The Haruspex will find the offering of the sheep's liver badly deformed at the ceremonies tomorrow. As you know, this frightening omen needs to be remedied swiftly. The High Priest will call for a pilgrimage to the sacred springs of Tinia at Monte Amiata to bring back its purified water to cleanse the altar. I have made arrangements that you will be among those chosen. You will fall deathly ill along the journey as you near Tressia, and you will be brought there to be healed.

Are you sure all of this has been arranged?

Yes, my priestess, I have been busy, and it is all set to happen according to our plan.

How can you be so sure?

Because I will be joining you on your journey, priestess, the one who will be guiding your coach on your pilgrimage. Of course, do not let on that we know each other.

Nico, I am so glad you are here.

I will be glad also when I get you back home safely.

City of Tressia, Home of Toscano

Gia, what's wrong? Gia?

Toscano, it is time, hurry, get Vera and the midwife, be quick, our baby is coming.

Toscano, you have a son Toscano, a healthy, newborn son.

Praise to the gods, a healthy son. I am blessed.

Gia, how is she?

She is weak but going to be fine, go, be with her and your new son.

You have a boy, Toscano.

The gods are good to me, a healthy boy and wife.

Here, go ahead and hold your son. Let him get to know who his father is.

He's so tiny.

He'll soon grow to be as strong as his father.

Stronger, he'll do remarkable things. What shall we call him?

What do you think about naming it after my father, his grandfather?

Yes, we should honor him. There, there, little one, be happy now. You have a name, Donato, after your grandfather. He is smiling, looking down at you, and you will make him proud.

Look, he's smiling back. He likes that name.

CHAPTER 10: THE AMBUSH

The Chambers of King Altare

Darius, it is time. We move out tonight under cover of darkness, and we shall soon meet outside the gates of Tressia. Victory over Tressia will finally be ours.

To our victory, Darius!

To victory, Altare!

Tressia Militia Barracks

Commander, we have reports from our scouts that the Tarchina army has left the city and has separated here, just south of the Fosso River. The main army continued to march north following the Fichina River, but a smaller contingent followed a trail along the Fosso River.

Matteo, look. I have been studying this map. If their main army continues north along the Fichina River, they'll have to pass through the Poggio Fichina gorge. This pass is the best

location to ambush their army, positioning
infantry and archers here and here, on the
high ground, on either side. Our forward
cavalry would be located here, and a rear
cavalry would be positioned out of sight
behind them. The attack would be from three
sides when their forward guard reaches this
point. They will have no choice but to call for
a retreat, and when they do, they will turn
and run right into our cavalry, charging up
here from the south. There'll be no escape.

They will be crushed, Commander. But how
can we be sure the main army will continue
into the gorge?

Knowing King Altare, I'm sure they won't.

What do you mean, Commander?

He'll anticipate this trap and travel north by
an alternate route. One where he can remain
undetected right up to the outskirts of our
valley, even if it adds days to their journey.

Which route? I know no alternate routes
north to Tressia; the Lemon Forrest blocks
the way.

Does it?

You and I have spent much time roaming that
forest; no route passed through it. There's
nothing more than a few animal trails to
follow, and it would be almost impossible to
get an army through it.

Yes, it will be slow, challenging, and unexpected; that's precisely why King Altare will use it. Emerging from the forest, somewhere here, anticipating we were set to ambush him along the Fichina River, he would outflank us and be in a cunning position to attack the mostly unprotected Tressia.

I think you may be right, Commander. It makes the most sense, knowing King Altare.

So, we faint the move to Poggio Fichina, sending our cavalry and a company of infantry, but the bulk of our army is to remain in the city, ready and waiting for King Altare to attack.

 And what of the detachment following the Fosso River branch?

They will continue to follow the Fosso River route, bringing them to the northern end of our valley and placing them in a position to attack our north gate. They are likely to strike when the main army initiates their frontal assault. We position two companies of calvary hidden here undetected. Once they attack, they will surprise with an assault from behind.

Incredibly well-devised, Commander. It will take stealth and timing, but we will take them by complete surprise.

Bring in the officers, and we will coordinate all these plans.

The Walls of Tressia

Archers ready, fire! Javelins ready, fire! Light the fires! Launch the flames!

Commander, they're retreating from the walls; some are already breaking and leaving the battle.

Attack with our cavalry, now.

It is over, Commander. Those still alive have surrendered and are laying down their arms.

Matteo, have you found King Darius?

Yes, Commander, over here, he's dead. It's over. Where is their King? Bring King Altare to me.

He managed to escape with the core of his cavalry, Commander.

Chambers of King Altare

Cintello, how many men have returned to the
city?

So far, fifty or so, my lord. Many of the
injured were taken prisoner.

Any reports on King Darius?

My lord, word has gotten back that they were
ambushed from behind. They say he was
surrounded and fought bravely right to the
end.

Cintello. They knew when we were coming.
They knew in advance our every move. I will
not rest until we discover exactly how this
happened, how they knew.

My lord, I suspect they have spies right here
within the city.

I want them found, and I will kill them myself. Do whatever it takes

Yes, my lord, I will.

Chambers of King Acri

My lord, King Altare has accepted our offer for a prisoner exchange.

Good, send him a message that we will arrive in two days and have the payment ready in gold.

Commander, did our spy among the prisoners suggest a captive to approach?

He did, my lord. He is a veteran of many battles. He goes by the name of Battista. He is bitter, tired of seeing his friends being killed in the foolish wars brought by his king.

We must speak to him without raising suspicion. Have our spy secretly contact this man Battista and tell him there is a way for him to stop the killing and let him know that I wish to speak to him. If he is willing to meet, I have a plan. Late tonight, he is to begin to cry out from a pain in his stomach, convulsing on his knees in anguish. Our spy yells to the guards to inform them that this man needs help. He is dying in pain. The guards are to drag him out of the cell and bring him to me. He will become our new contact in the city for Cristo.

Chamber of King Acri, Two Months Later

Has our friendly merchant brought us news?

Yes, my lord, Cristo has returned from Tarchina with a message from our contact Battista. He mentioned that the noble most suspect of King Altare is a landowner, wealthy wine trader, and newly elected Princeps Civitatis of the council of elders, the Larth Arnthal.

Perfect, he will have much influence. Find out whom he deals with at the port of Tarquinii. He must be starting the trading of harvest soon. We are in the market for many amphoras of wine, and he will quickly become our leading supplier. Go to Tarquinii and inquire about him.

Yes, my lord, I will leave at once.

My lord, I am told the wine trader, the Larth Arnthal sets up shop directly across from the harbor. He is expected there shortly.

Good, I am getting thirsty, Toscano. Let's buy some wine.

Port of Tarquinii

Your majesty, would you care for a sample of this season's vintage? It has been one of my finest.

You must say that every season.

99

I just may, your majesty, but I am sure you will be pleased.

It is a fine wine. How many amphoras do you have with you?

Give me a moment, your majesty, and I will check my storage room.

Of course.

I have twenty-two amphoras remaining, your majesty.

I will buy the entire lot.

All twenty-two?

Yes, all of them.

Thank you, your majesty. I'm glad you find the wine so pleasing.

You know your king will soon learn that you trade with his enemy.

I pay him enough in taxes, your majesty, so it should not matter how I source my funds.

In my case, it will.

He is my King, but that does not give him the liberty to approve my every transaction.

He takes liberties, Larth, along with many lives to which he has no right.

There is truth in what you say, your majesty, and many of Tarchina are no longer pleased with him.

Are there members of the council who feel this way?

There are, your majesty, and our feelings are more substantial since the disastrous war with you. Many have lost loved ones, including myself, and there is little patience to endure much more from this king.

If these voices ring loud enough, I will hear them. I am ready to aid the council if called. Be assured, Larth Arnthal, that I'm not expecting payment in return. Tarchina will remain a free and independent city. My reward will be to see the people of Tarchina rid of this tyrant. Larth, the citizens of Tarchina must rise and end this cruel and devious reign.

Your majesty, you speak of treason. A dangerous step that I am not willing to take.

When you are, Larth Arnthal, know I am willing to help.

Your majesty, that time may never come, but if by chance it does, how may I contact you again?

The wine flows freely in Tressia, and I will seek more of your wine regularly.

CHAPTER 12: THE CONSPIRACY

Home of Larth Arnthal, City of Tarchina

I see you have returned from Tarquinii with a wagon full of supplies. Your trading must have been beneficial.

It was Marcus due to one very lucrative transaction.

Tell me, so I may also enjoy some of this lucrative trading.

Marcus, this transaction was with someone the king is not very fond of and included more than just wine.

Now I am curious. You must tell me.

Come, let's speak together while we walk. It's a beautiful night to enjoy the cool evening breeze and gaze upon the stars.

Arnthal, why such caution? What is this all about?

Even at home, the walls have ears, my friend, and what I am about to say must remain between us.

Now, what is this about?

It's about someone powerful with the means and concern to aid us.

Aid us in doing what?

We are freeing the people of Tarchina.

My god, Arnthal, what are you saying? Just mentioning such a thing could get us both killed. You know this, King; he has executed for less.

It is time we act, Marcus.

Stop, no more of this talk. I do not want to know who this man is or what he can do.

It is King Altare of Tressia.

King Altare? Did you trade your amphoras of wine with King Altare?

Yes, he bought all I had. A wagon full of wine travels to Tressia as we speak.

If King Altare finds out about this, there is no telling what he might do.

I trade with a king who has the means to make the purchase. If he wants his taxes, he cannot interfere.

You know he can, and if he learns who it is, there is no telling what he will do.

Marcus, we can no longer live under this tyrant and must act soon.

Arnthal, I am not willing to participate in whatever you are planning. It's far too dangerous. He is king and remains in control of everything.

He is not in control of everything.

Larth, no, no more of this. You talk of treason. You are the newly elected Princeps Civitatis of the council of Elders to the King, second in power only to him. His trusted advisor. Your loyalty is expected. If he discovers your talk of betrayal, he will have you killed. You, of all people, know this, Arnthal. He has done exactly that many times before.

You know the king as well as I do. He doesn't listen to me or any of us. He only hears himself; the will of the people be damned. Marcus, you know many feel as we do and are ready. The time to act is upon us.

Arnthal, what have you done? Who besides King Altare have you spoken to about this?

I have done nothing but listen.

Listened to whom? Who else?

To General Pulenas, after the ambush at Poggio Fichina. His army is in ruins. They blame King Altare for the massacre and for leading his man into a trap. He has told me he would move on the King if he knew the council would follow.

A coup? A military coup and they want your help. Is this what this is all about?

He is waiting for our word that the council will join him. Marcus, if you support me, we will turn the tide and end this reign. You know this is the only way, and now is the time to strike. Marcus, are you with me?

Larth, this is risky business. If anything goes wrong, we are both dead, and there must be a better, less dangerous way.

Marcus, look at me. You must call upon your courage. I know you can, Marcus. We have known each other since we were boys, and you have the courage. We must do this together, for Tarchina. This rule must be ended.

I need time to think. Let me go. If I'm involved, it needs to be done right, or everyone involved will die. The king has spies everywhere.

Marcus, think about this quickly. The longer we wait, the more danger we face.

We will speak tomorrow. Meet me at the market at noon.

The Market at Tarchina

I hear the dates are delicious now. The gods have been generous this season. Here, try one. Sweet, isn't it?

Yes, they are.

Let me buy you a dozen. Let's go. I know just the place to sit and enjoy them; fruit always tastes better in a garden.

Larth, I have thought hard about what we spoke about, and I have a plan.

I am glad, Marcus, for us and the city of Tarchina, it will be a proper place to live again.

Arnthal, it must be done on the field of battle where suspicion will fall on no one. Only then will your ascension onto the throne be legitimate, fairly elected by the Council of Elders.

Marcus, it sounds excellent, my friend. How does this get done?

That is where we need King Acri. He needs to prepare an attack on the city to finish the war started by King Altare. Our General Pulenas will devise a plan to surprise the enemy as they camp on their way to the city. A fitting reprisal for the ambush at Poggio Fichina. But the army of Tressia will be ready and waiting for the raid with a marksman positioned, ready to quickly put an end to our King.

Excellent, my friend. It will take preparation, but it is well-conceived. I must get word to King Acri about what is expected of him. Once it is agreed upon, we will get the details to General Pulenas.

Arnthal, no matter how well-conceived, putting it in action is still extremely dangerous.

It is a risk worth taking. We will speak again once we get word to King Acri.

How will you reach him?

I have ways.

Be careful. Our lives depend upon it.

I will, my friend. Enjoy your dates. We will speak again soon.

CHAPTER 13: A FITTING REPRISAL

Port of Tarquinii

Your majesty, is it time for more wine?

It is, Larth. Do you have anything interesting for us?

I do. It's back here in my storage room. Please follow me.

Toscano, come, let's sample what Larth has held in storage.

Certainly, your majesty, we have enjoyed what Larth has sold us.

Look here on the map. Do you know this fortress on the edge of the Lemon Forest called Rofalco?

Yes, it is within the territory of the city of Vulci.

I know it also. It is a two-day march from Tressia, and the city sometimes uses it to control the route to Lake Mezzano.

That is where you are to set camp on your way to attack Tarchina.

Attack Tarchina?

Yes, that is our plan. The king is to be killed, leading an ambush of your camp at Rofalco. Our general, Aquila Pulenas, has joined us and planned the ambush at Rofalco.

It does make sense for us to set camp there, your majesty. It's a defendable position for our army on the way to attack Tarchina.

Tells more of this plan.

He will be prepared to attack before dawn once he receives word that you have set camp at the fortress. He and the King will lead the attack and approach here at this east wall. You will be waiting and position a sharpshooter here so that he will have a clear shot at the King.

Do you trust this general?

I do. The general has spent thirty years in the service of Tarchina. He despises this King and what he has caused to happen to his army, and he will do his part without question.

How will the King be spotted at night?

He will be easy to spot. He'll be wearing his battle armor, a bronze chest plate draped with a red cape and bloomed helmet. The difficulty will be landing an arrow precisely. Only the front of the neck is exposed, so it must strike his throat below his helmet. It is an exacting strike, made even more so since he will ride on horseback at night.

I know of a man who has trained his life for a strike such as this.

Good, then it is agreed.

Larth, what will the council do once they learn their King is dead? Whom will they choose as a successor?

Nothing is certain, your majesty.

I hear you are the most likely.

I am ready if called upon, your majesty.

Good Larth, modesty is a worthy attribute of a future king. To our success, then, to a new era for Tarchina! Long live the new King!

The Fortress of Rafalco

Matteo, it won't be long now. They will be approaching right towards you.

I am set, Commander. It is as good as done.

110

Wait, behind us, did you hear that? We are being attacked from behind; It's a trap. Matteo, we will soon be surrounded. Quickly gather the men. We must break out together right now.

Chambers of King Altare

Is it done, Cintello?

Yes, my lord. Our Princeps Civitatis will not be causing you any more problems.

Did we learn all we needed to know?

We did, and more.

And of the General?

He did the honorable thing, my lord, and took his own life with his sword.

And of the army of Tressia?

The battle rages as we speak, my lord.

Bring word to me from Commander Persena as soon as you hear.

Yes, my lord. Is there anything else?

Yes, excellent work, Cintello. You and our new Princeps Civatis Marcus will be rewarded handsomely.

Thank you, my lord.

The Fortress of Rafalco

Commander, your shoulder is injured.

I will be fine. Keep the men moving. We must gain distance from them before dawn.

You must rest, Commander, and dress that wound.

Listen, do you hear that?

A stream?

Yes, it's not far. Let's head to it. The water will cover our tracks and lead us to the coast. Have the men traveled within the stream? If it deepens, we can use branches and logs to help us float downstream.

Commander, we are heading in the direction of Vulci, and this must be a branch of the Olpeta River.

Good, we will be safe within the city. Once we are there, we can get word back to Tressia. I hope their king remembers us from the festival at Fanum Voltumnae.

I hope so. Unfortunately, the king enjoyed himself too much and was mainly drunk.

Matteo, do you hear that? Matteo, swim for the bank! Matteo!

Men go to the bank quickly. The current will pull you over the falls.

Matteo, are you hurt?

No, commander, I am fine. Fortunately, that pond was deep. I would even do it again if we didn't have an army chasing after us.

Chambers of King Acri

Nico, what news do we have from our scouts?

It is not good news, your majesty.

Tell me, what have they seen?

There was a brutal battle, your majesty, at Rafalco, and there is no sign of our men. They must have retreated into the forest.

King Altare must have uncovered our plan. We must find them. Nico, go with a company of men and find them, and be careful.

I will find them, your majesty.

CHAPTER 14: VULCI

Guard post outside the City of Vulci

Stop! You men there, stop! Not a step further!
Lay down your weapons.

Sir, I am commander Tuscano of Tressia, and
these are my men. We are escaping capture
by the army of Tarchina. Please take me to
your king.

Escaping? I see; follow me.

The Vulci Stockade

Guard, what are you doing? I told you; I am
Commander Toscano of Tressia. I am here to
see your king.

And I am the god Larce, guardian of the
travelers. Now, all of you, get inside!

You, guard, you must take this decree from
King Acri to your king. We are here seeking
sanctuary. He will remember us. I am
Commander Toscano of Tressia, and this is
my general, Matteo of Vacalvi. We guarded

him at the festival. You must tell him we are
here.

Did you say Matteo? Matteo of Vacalvi?

Yes, he is here.

Bring him forward.

I am Matteo of Vacalvi, now a general of
Tressia. The commander speaks the truth.

Matteo, don't you recognize me? It's me,
Tarsus.

Tarsus? By the grace of the gods, it is you.
You are alive!

Alive and well, my friend. I cannot believe my
eyes after all this time. Matteo, what are you
doing here?

Well, get us out of here, and I'll tell you.

Chambers of King Vel Saties

I owe you and your men an apology,
commander. My guards woefully neglected to
inform me of your identity. I am so sorry that
we treated you and your men so harshly.

 Understandable, given our appearance and
our unexpected entrance to your city. No
harm done, your majesty.

You and your general are to be my guests at a
banquet tonight.

Thank you, your majesty.

In the meantime, I will have all of you
appropriately dressed.

That is exceedingly kind of you, your majesty.
If I may, I have an urgent request.

Yes, of course, commander.

Can I send a message to my king, telling him
of our safe arrival here in Vulci and our
imminent return to Tressia?

Consider it done, commander.

The Army Barracks of Vulci

Matteo, I'm still amazed to see you alive, or
should I say, General Matteo.

Tarsus, for you, it will always be just Matteo,
as it was in our youth in Vacalvi.

Those days seem so long ago now, and I
cannot believe it is gone, the whole city of
Vacalvi abandoned.

I made it back there, returning after our exile.
It was heartbreaking, nothing like the city we
left. Famine and disease engulfed the city.
Starvation, death, and disease were
everywhere. King Darius was desperate; near
the end, he had the army raiding the
countryside, scavenging for supplies. Those
remaining were killing and stealing to

116

survive. A total collapse and exodus came at the end. You are lucky you did not see it.

And what of the people that survived? Where did they go?

Those that were able headed for Tressia to start a new life there.

Your family, did they survive?

Only my brother Janus was among those who endured. He is with me now in Tressia.

And what of Larce? Is he alive? Have you seen him?

I did see him weeks after we separated. He never made it out of the forest, Tarsus, and he had plunged down a steep ravine and now sleeps with the gods.

Poor Larce, he was a faithful friend to both of us. We all thought we would stay friends forever and live as soldiers of Vacalvi.

Our destiny would not have it so, but it brought the two of us back together now.

It did so, and I am grateful for that. Tell me, Matteo, how is it possible that you have become a great general of Tressia?

I will, but first, you must tell me of your life here in Vulci.

Well, where should I start? Initially, it was hard, but the skills we learned as children training in Vacalvi have served me well. Do you remember those days, Matteo, and our teacher, Horace?

Of course, how could I forget? You were so clumsy and slow at first, a pond turtle, barely getting out of your own way.

Ah, you were so frail you could not pull back your first training bow until you were seven.

I was eight. Those were hard but meaningful days, my friend,

They were, and it is all gone now.

Are you happy here, Tarsus? Do you live alone, or have you met someone?

I have indeed met someone; she is the love of my life. Her name is Thalia. You must meet her. She has the beauty of a goddess and a heart of gold.

I am happy for you, Tarsus. The gods have been generous to us. Tarsus, you must come back with me to Tressia. You will have a place in our army. It is a fine city and one that can always use a man of your talent. You and your wife Thalia, you must come. You will live happily there.

My friend, I wish, but my life is here now, and Thalia, she carries our child.

Tarsus, you are to be a father; you will make a fine one. May the gods continue their blessings and give you a healthy child.

I am blessed, Matteo, and grateful to the gods for allowing us to see each other again.

It has been a blessing knowing that you are alive, my friend. May the gods allow our paths to cross again.

Chambers of King Vel Saties

Your majesty, I thank you for your hospitality. I am most indebted to you.

Safe journey to you, Toscano, and give my regards to your king. Let him know I cherish the bond between our two cities.

I will, your majesty, and may the gods continue to bestow favor upon you and your city.

CHAPTER 15: THE HUNT

The Lemon Forest

Commander, we found them camped about two miles to the northeast.

Good, encircle them, and this time no one gets away.

There, just up ahead, Commander.

Silvius, move in, now, carefully, take them by surprise.

Lay down your arms now, or you all shall die!

Who are these men? Where is Toscano?

Commander, this is a company of men from Tressia sent out to find and rescue Toscano and his men.

Kill them. We cannot be escorting captives. We need to find Toscano!

Wait, commander, I recognize this one from when our militia was in Tressia. It is Nico, Toscano's younger brother.

Well, that changes things. Bring him with us.
He may be useful to our king. Kill the rest.

Chambers of King Acri

Toscano, it is good to see you alive. King
Altare uncovered our plot, and he killed all
those who were involved. It is a miracle that
you and your men made it out alive.

Without the aid of King Val Saties, all would
have been lost. He gave us refuge in the city
and fresh horses for our return here.

We owe him much in the way of gratitude.

Which we certainly will repay. Now, what of
Nico?

What do you mean, my lord?

You don't know? I sent Nico to find you when
I received reports of you and your men
escaping the attack at Rafalco. Nico was
captured searching for you and is held for
ransom in Tarchina.

Your majesty, I must leave at once and rescue
him.

Toscano, you mustn't be rash. As you can
attest, King Altare has proven to be an astute
and cunning opponent. We have failed to
outmaneuver him in the past, costing us
many lives. It may be best to agree to his
demands and pay the ransom; an

opportunity will arise to avenge this extortion.

I do not trust him, my lord. Even if we do pay, will he uphold his end of the bargain? We must find a way to rescue him.

Let us give it time. If we attempt a rescue, it must be cleverly conceived and expertly executed, or once again, many will die at the hands of King Altare.

There is someone who may be able to help us. Someone as concerned as you for Nico's safe return. Someone who has inside knowledge of the workings of the court of Tarchina and, most importantly, has the complete confidence of King Altare.

That could only be one person, the High Priest Jovan.

Yes, he is perfect, and it is time for him to make his round to Tarchina.

City of Tarchina Prison House

What have we here?

His name is Custos. He is accused of attacking and raping a barmaid at the tavern.

It looks like she got the best of him.

No, not her, sir. He wouldn't come peacefully, so the guards had to do some convincing.

What a stench! He is filthy and drunk. Throw
him in the last cell with the other prisoner.
Be sure he is cleaned up by morning before
facing the magistrate. I don't want that
stench smelling up the court.

Yes, sir, I will see to it.

Sir, the prisoner, you must see this.

What is it? Why is your face covered?

The Death, sir, the prisoner has pus marks on
his face and arms. The other prisoner, too,
sir, and it's already spreading.

Lock up the prison house. Everyone out! Get
out! Everyone! Now, out!

Chambers of King Altare

Your majesty, the warden reports that two
prisoners have the pustules, the plague, your
majesty, and he has sealed the prison house.

Is he sure?

He says he is sure. He's seen it before.

The prisoners he speaks of, is one of them
Nico, the brother of Toscano?

I'm afraid so, your majesty. He's infected.

Bring me the high priest, now.

Jovan, there's an outbreak of the plague in
prison. The city must be spared. What can be

done to appease the gods and stop the spread?

How many have the pustules, your majesty?

There are two, the two prisoners being held there.

The gods must be outraged to bring this horror upon Tarchina. We must act quickly before the plague spreads death throughout the city.

Where are the prisoners now? Have they been expelled?

The prison house has been sealed with the two prisoners inside.

They need to be expelled, at once, your majesty. They must not die within the city walls, or the city will undoubtedly be cursed. They must be bound and covered from head to toe and brought to the necropolis. They must be buried while still alive, in one grave. It must be done before sunset; it is the only way the gods will be appeased.

It will be done.

Necropolis of Tarchina

Can you hear me, Nico?

Toscano, I can hardly breathe.

Stay calm, Nico. Matteo will dig us out as soon as it's clear.

124

Toscano, I can't see. I can't breathe and can hardly move.

Nico, be calm and take slow, even breaths. It won't be long now. Try to put your mind at ease. Nico, remember when we were in a tough spot when we were young? We would get through it by sticking together.

No, I can't think. I can't.

Yes, you can. Think back and try to remember a time.

My dawning?

Yes, you found the strength, then.

With your help. And we were both almost killed.

Yes, but we did it together, and we'll do this together. Do you hear me, Nico? Nico? Listen, Nico, I hear them. They're digging.

Quick, get Nico, hurry, get that sack off him! Nico! Wake up! Nico? Praise the gods. Breathe, Nico, breathe.

Matteo, you are a welcome sight.

It's good to see you too, Commander, but you look terrible.

Glad to be alive. Now, let's get out of here before we're seen.

Vera, how is Nico back there?

He said you gave him the plague and buried him alive, so he is not too happy with you.

I see. You didn't tell him that this was all your idea.

No, I'm giving you all the credit, Commander.

Matteo, are you sure this wagon will make it back to Tressia?

Not sure about that. We'll see how far we get.

The further we get away from Tarchina, the better I'll feel. Once the king discovers we're

gone, he'll send his whole army after us.

Hopefully, we will be in Tressia by that time.

Well, pick up the pace, Matteo, and let's increase those odds.

CHAPTER 16: VILLA FEONIA

Chambers of King Acri

Commander, please come. I have something I would like to show you here on this map. Look right here, this hill, see how it is positioned overlooking the surrounding countryside and the river Osborne and across the valley to Tressia. Notice also how it lies alongside the metal-bearing Colline Metallifere.

Yes, your majesty. I know that area well, and the village of Murlo is nearby.

When was the last time you were in this area?

It must be at least two years ago, your majesty. I traveled those hills collecting copper and silver ore for my father's kiln.

Well, it has changed much since then. This hilltop is now the site of the Villa of Feonia, named in honor of our queen.

A new villa for your majesty?

127

No, not for me, and it will be more than a villa. When finished, it will be an expansive compound having a residence, temple, banquet hall, courtyard, extensive workshops, and more.

My lord, it is well-positioned, but it is exposed, with no natural barriers for protection.

That is one reason I called you here, Toscano. I want your recommendations for securing the compound.

I understand, your majesty. May I spend some time reviewing the plan before I give my suggestions?

Take all the time you need, Toscano. My master-builder, Pesna, knows my vision for Feonia and will explain what is to be done there. You are to collaborate with him closely.

Yes, your majesty. If I may, it will aid me in planning if I know who will live there.

When completed, it is to be the home to the commander of the army of Tressia while serving his king. It will be a far more proper place for you and your growing family.

You're most generous, Majesty.

You earned it, Commander, sealed with your superb victory over King Altare.

The Villa Feonia

The view from the crest of the hilltop was spectacular. The landscape was filled with gently sloping hills as far as the eye could see. The hills were once entirely blanketed by a cover of thick forest, but now they are punctuated by scattered fields of green and golden brown, separated by lines of towering cypresses. Off in the distance, I could see the outline of Tressia rising on the opposing mountainside. It was simple to know why the king had chosen this place to find his new villa of Feonia.

Matteo, where do you think we should find the watchtowers?

One here, Pesna, on the north side of the villa, to form this corner. The other is to be here on the south side, set further up the slope and built to a height of at least thirty feet. Anything less, the view of the lower valley below and the river Osborne would be obstructed. And it would be best if it connected the tower to the villa's south wall with a colonnade, creating a passageway back to the estate. The south tower would also anchor this corner of the fenced field surrounding the southern section.

Yes, that would make sense, and if the colonnade were to be enclosed, it would make an ideal location to house the scouts and militia stationed here.

Good, let's go and discuss these thoughts with the King.

So, here it is, Gia, the home of the commander of the army of Tressia, our new home.

Oh, my gods, it's stunning, Toscano, much more than I could have ever imagined. It is going to be so wonderful living here. Just look at the size of this place. How are we going to fill it all?

We have craftsmen who can build us all the furniture and furnishing we need. I don't think it will take you long to make it feel like home. See the kitchen and banquet hall; they are almost complete and right over here. Now look at that far end of the courtyard; that's where the Temple will be. The castings of the roof sculptures are being completed in the workshop. The Temple entrance will be right here, with steps leading up to the podia.

Toscano, this villa is immense.

It is. And the vision the king has for this place goes beyond a residence and Temple. The king wants it to be completely self-sufficient, producing all the items we need right here, with all the raw materials we need, from the clay for the roofing tiles to the stone, wood, and metal for the construction, which is easily sourced right here in the valley. He is also expecting it to have the ability to manufacture goods for trade with the surrounding countryside and to supply necessities to Tressia.

Toscano, this is so impressive. I can see the artisans have already done extraordinary work to bring it to life.

They have. Pesna has assembled the finest artisans from as far away as Venezia, including my father and Janus, Matteo's brother. Look at the finishing on the head of that terracotta roof tile here. That is a sculpture of the god Satyr, one of my favorites.

Remarkable.

Adrian did it. He's an expert craftsman, known to be one of the finest sculptors in all of Etruria. He also did that roof tile with the head of a maenad. Just in case there is any doubt about whose work this is, Adrian inscribes his unique mark, the letter Alpha with a descending medial bar, on the back surface of all his work.

Inside was impressive. The entire villa seemed full of life. The hallways and rooms were brightly painted and adorned with intricate colored motifs. Plenty of construction left to be done, but when completed, it will certainly be a fitting monument to our queen.

With construction nearing completion, the king planned a great ceremonial banquet to thank the gods, honor the queen, and impress his nobles and guests. He arranged a staff of over twenty servants to cater to the affair. The king's entourage arrived just as the

finishing decorations were added to the
banquet room.

A traveling troop of dancers, musicians,
singers, and entertainers accompanied them.
When it was time for the festivities to begin,
the entire banquet hall was filled. Every
couch, lounge chair, and mat was fully
occupied.

The seating was arranged around the wall, so
everyone faced each other, with low, three-
legged dining tables placed in front of them.
The king and queen were seated at the
center. Matteo, Nico, and I, along with Gia and
Vera, sat together near the entrance. We
could not help but feel slightly out of place in
such an opulent setting. The king did his best
to make us feel at ease, toasting our recent
victories at Poggio Fichina and Val Di Comino
and imploring the gods to continue our
success.

The diners were all exquisitely dressed for
the occasion. The rich and noble families of
Tressia, both men and women, wore
expensive woven linen robes and dresses.
The women were adorned with shimmering
gold and silver jewelry bands and bathed in
exotic perfumes. Soon an abundance of food
and drink began to appear. Trays made the
rounds of roasted meat, including beef, lamb,
deer, and boar. Fish of all kinds followed,
along with cheese, olives, fruit, eggs, nuts,
and raisins, were all paraded by the servants.

The feasting, drinking, music, and entertainment continued into the early morning. Eventually, some grew tired and slept right at their places. By early afternoon, the feasting renewed until no one could eat another morsel. The banquet only ended when the king had his fill and rose to his feet to bid everyone farewell, and the feast was officially over.

Many of the nobles were far too drunk to leave on their own. They had to be carried off to their waiting carriages by their servants for the short journey back to their villas. This banquet will not be forgotten.

CHAPTER 17: HE HAS RISEN

Chambers of King Altare

My lord, our spy servant, Vesia, in Tressia, has given us a puzzling report on a banquet celebrating the completion of a new villa in the hills outside Tressia.

Puzzling?

Yes, my Lord, it has not been confirmed, but she is reporting that Nico of Tressia, the brother of Commander Toscano, attended the banquet.

Nico of Tressia? The same Nico we buried alive, infected with the Black Death, that Nico?

Yes, my Lord. She's positive it was him, the brother of Toscano. They were at the banquet together, feasting side by side, all night; Nico, Toscano, his wife Gia, Vera, Gia's sister, and his second in command, Matteo of Vacalvi.

How is that possible? Did he rise from the dead? Go to the necropolis now, dig up those coffins and see if they are empty.

Yes, my Lord.

My Lord, the grave shows signs of having been disturbed, and the coffins were empty.

No wonder Tressia has not retaliated. We have been cleverly deceived, Cintello. Nico is alive and well, enjoying his freedom back in Tressia. Where exactly did you say this new villa was found?

Villa Feonia

Toscano, do you have to leave again so soon?

I will not be long now. The King has asked that Matteo and I go with him again to this year's festival at Fanum Voltumnae. Nico will remain stationed here with a full company of men. Gia, while I am gone, please don't leave the villa without him and two escort guards, even if it is only to the market.

Yes, commander. I'm missing you already.

It should be no longer than a week, Gia.

Oh, Toscano, be sure to bring back a present for Donato. His one-year birthday is approaching.

Village of Murlo

It is good to see you again. May I offer you a jar of our most refined olive oil or porcini mushrooms, perhaps? I know; here, try a piece of my goat cheese. It's delicious when served with sweet wine.

No, thank you, where are your lentils? Our cook sent me here specifically for them.

Yes, they are right back here. Here let me help you.

The Commander leaves for Fanum Voltumnae tomorrow. He is expected to be gone for at least a week.

Here, take this. It is a special gift. I need you to do me a favor.

What may I ask?

Tomorrow night at the south tower, the guard on midnight duty must be completely distracted as he starts his shift and ensures he remains so for a while.

Why? What is happening tomorrow night?

That is not of your concern. Look at what I have wrapped for you. That's your only concern.

This is my concern. It is much more than I agreed to do. If I am to agree to do this, I must know why.

You ask for too much, Vesia. It's you who should be informing me.

You must be mistaken; this package isn't for me.

Wait, it's a going-away present. It is yours.

Tell me what this is all about, or you can keep your present.

The guard at the south tower must not be aware of the mercenaries trying to enter the villa.

Mercenaries? Is it gold and jewelry they desire?

Only they know what they seek.

Where are they from?

I know they will return to Corsica once they have what they want. That's all I know. Are you satisfied now? Do we have a deal? Will you keep that guard distracted for a while?

Be assured; that he'll be very distracted for a while.

It's been nice doing business with you, Vesia.

Villa Feonia

The baby, my lady, he's up. He needs to be fed.

Now, my little tiger, I'm right here, little one. Now, it's time to lie back down so I can get back to sleep. You were so hungry.

Who's there? What are you doing? Leave me alone!

My lady, may I come in? Are you all right, my lady? My lady? Oh, my gods! She's gone! Vera! Nico! Come quick! It's my lady! She's gone!

Vesia, where's Gia? What are you saying? Look at me. Tell me what has happened. Where is she?

I don't know. I just heard her call out. It came from the bedroom. She was there, in the bedroom.

Tell me, what did you hear? Vesia, think, what did you hear?

I don't know. My poor lady. My poor lady.

Vesia, look at me. Take a breath. Vesia, look at me and tell me what just happened. Slowly now, what did you hear?

I first heard the baby. He needed to be fed. I awoke my lady, and she went in to nurse him, and now she's gone! She cried out and told them to stop. They have taken her.

Who took her, Vesia? What did you see?

I don't know. I don't know. I didn't see anything. She's gone, my poor lady, she's gone.

Fanum Voltumnae Fairgrounds

Your majesty, a rider from Tressia, carries troubling news.

Excuse me, gentleman, the burden of a king never ceases.

Your majesty, the Lady Gia, she's gone. She's been taken.

What do you mean by taking?

Kidnapped, your majesty, during the night from the villa.

When was this?

Two nights ago, your majesty.

Was anyone seen?

No, your majesty, her house servant heard a disturbance, and she was gone.

Find Toscano and bring him to me at once.

Yes, your majesty.

Toscano, I'm afraid I just received horrid news from Tressia.

What is it, my lord?

Lady Gia has been abducted.

Gia? What do you mean abducted? Where is she? When? My Gia?

Toscano, we will find her. We'll leave at once.
Toscano, wait, where are you going?

I must find her now!

Wait, Toscano, you will need my help.
Together...Toscano! Wait!

Matteo, Gia has been abducted. I must leave
at once; you must stay with the king.

Commander, wait, I will go with you.

No, stay with the king. I will contact you as
soon as I can.

Commander, be careful. You know who is
behind this.

Villa Feonia

Toscano, we heard nothing.

Where's my son? Nico! Where's my son?

He is safe, unharmed, in his nursery, with
Vesia.

Tell me what you know, everything Nico,
from the beginning. How did they get in?
How many were they?

Toscano, I'm so sorry. I'm so sorry I didn't
stop it. I didn't protect her. It's my fault she is
gone. It's all my fault.

No. Nico, I'm not blaming you. It's not your
fault. Now tell me what you know. I need to

know everything if I am to get her back. Everything you know. Now, how did they get in?

I'll show you. It was through this entrance here we found the door pried open. They left these marks here on the frame.

Who was the guard duty there in the south tower that night?

First, 'till midnight, it was Arnza, and then, until first light, it was Sepia.

Bring them to me. I will speak to each of them separately.

Arnza, tell me what happened on the night Gia was abducted. Everything you saw. I need to know everything.

Commander, it was a regular post, nothing unusual to report.

Tell me what you saw, starting right when your shift began, from moment to moment.

Right before dark, I saw Ramu driving the sheep inside the gate. Once the dogs were inside, he closed the side gates behind him. Then he drove them into their pen and headed to the barracks.

Then what?

As I said, Commander, it was a quiet night. Nothing really to report.

Nothing else? No one else was about?

No, no one outside the gates, commander.

What about inside the gates? What did you see? Did you see anyone else in the south yard?

No one unusual, I swear, Commander.

I want to know everything you saw, everything. Whom did you see?

Later, I did see a servant from the kitchen. She tossed the waste from the evening meal into the pigpen and then fetched some water.

Which servant?

Vesia, I believe. It was dark by then, Commander. The moon was not yet up, but it looked like her, it's a distance, Commander, but it did look like her.

Was there anyone with her? Did you see her with someone else?

No, she came out alone.

No one else? Think, you didn't see her with anyone?

No. Wait, I did see Sepia go over to her before he came up to relieve me. They spoke for a moment.

For how long? How long were they speaking?

Not long, Commander. It couldn't have been more than a few words, just a few words.

Then he headed up to the tower to relieve me.

And the rest of the evening, what else did you see?

There was nothing else, Commander. I swear. That's all I saw right up to when Sepia relieved me. Nothing else, inside the compound or out. I am confident, Commander.

Arnza, if anything else comes to mind, find me at once. Anything could be significant.

I will, commander. I am sorry I was not of more help, and I am sorry for what happened to my lady. I am sure you will get her back, Commander. I'm sure of it.

Thank you, Arnza. I will. Now, have Sepia come in.

Sepia, sit, sit down. I need to know everything that happened the night my lady was abducted: everything, Sepia, the truth, all of it. Now tell me what happened. Start right when you left the barracks to begin your shift.

Nothing happened, Commander. It was quiet all night. There was nothing to report. By the time my shift started, no one was around, nothing to see my whole time on shift.

Were you on the lookout the whole time? The whole night? You never took your eyes off your watch?

I was on watch the whole shift. I never left my post, Commander, never.

I know about that servant girl Vesia, Sepia. I know you spoke to her before your shift started. Now tell me what was said before I go and ask her myself.

She offered to bring me some soup from the kitchen, Commander.

Soup?

Yes, soup, Commander. It gets cold in the tower.

And then what happened? The truth Sepia, all of it. This is the last time I am asking. It was more than just soup.

She wouldn't stop, Commander. I told her she had to leave, but she wouldn't. She started talking and wouldn't stop. Finally, I tried to push her out and force her to go, but she just came closer and closer.

Sepia, how long was she with you in the tower? How long was she there, Sepia?

It wasn't long, Commander, and she left right after. She wasn't there that long.

Did you see or hear anything outside the compound while you were with her?

No, nothing, Commander.

Think hard, Sepia. For my wife, think hard before you answer.

144

I'm not sure, but I think I did hear something. I am not sure what it was. It was faint. But it did sound like horses off in the distance.

Where did it come from?

I couldn't see, but it seemed to come from the north, in the direction of the road.

How many do you think it was?

One or two. It was only for an instant; then, it was gone.

What have you said to Vesia since that night?

Nothing, Commander, nothing, she won't even look at me. I have no use for her. I let you down, Commander. It's my fault she's gone, and I don't deserve to serve you any longer.

Sepia, your weakness has caused great harm. You must be disciplined for this failure. But your honesty, just now, has saved your life. You will be punished but will serve me again.

You honor me, Commander.

Go now, Sepia, and be ready for what I may ask of you.

I will be ready, Commander. I will never let you down again.

Nico, find that servant girl Vesia and bring her to me.

Toscano, they say she left for the market in Murlo soon after you arrived.

We need to find her now!

The Market of Murlo

Fapi, the Commander, has returned. He's already interrogating the guards and will be looking for me next. He's going to find out about what I did, and he'll find out about everything, including you. I have all the money you gave me; we must leave now while we still can.

Now?

Yes, right now! He will be coming after me.

All right. I know the ship in Vulci the mercenaries will be using. It may still be there. I can help you buy your passage. It'll take you to Vulci. You'll be safe there.

Good, let's go.

I need to pack up the wagon before we can go.

No Fapi, now! There's no time for that. Leave everything. Fapi, cover everything and let's go. Hurry, if he finds us here, he will kill us both. We need to go! Now!

Have you seen the servant girl, Vesia, from my villa?

Yes, Commander, she was just here a few moments ago. She was heading to buy her produce. She was in a hurry.

Buy from whom?

From a merchant at the other end of the market. He is just down there. His name is Fapi. Wait, I don't see him. He was there a moment ago.

Nico, quickly, they can't be far.

There, up ahead, Toscano, that wagon, it must be them.

Stop! Get down, the both of you. Get down now!

Where are you taking her? Talk, or I shall slit your throat right here.

Wait, I'll tell you.

Everything or you die right here. Now, who sent you?

Toscano! The dagger! Watch out!

Give me the name. Tell me who, and the gods will reward you.

Altare.

Where? Where is she? Tell me, where?

He's dead, Toscano. He's gone.

Bind the girl and put her in the wagon. She'll tell us all we need to know.

Villa Feonia

Vesia tells us the truth of what you know, and I shall let you live.

Live? Why? So, I will serve you or another master, a house servant, a slave girl, for the rest of my life. That is not a life I want to live.

You have been treated well, Vesia. A member of our household. A trusted member.

A member of your household? You mean a servant girl, a slave in your home, doing what she is told daily with no end.

There is an end for you, as for all good servants. A day will come when you will be given the freedom and ability to lead a life of your choosing.

A day will come. I've heard those words before from other masters, including the king. Yet here I am, a slave girl serving my next master. I am tired of waiting for that day, and I have chosen to take my destiny into my own hands.

So, you betrayed us, allowing my wife to be taken from me, her child, and her life here. Abducted so you could buy your freedom.

I did not know they were here after her. But now she knows what it feels like to be a slave.

She is no slave, so she doesn't deserve to be a slave.

Neither did I, yet here I am. Sold into slavery by my father so our family would have a place to live and food to eat and continue to serve the king.

Enslaving someone else to save yourself is no better than those who enslaved you. It must be stopped, Vesia. Tell me what you know, make this right, and we will help each other.

Why should I trust you? You are no different from any of them. Why should I believe you?

Because you know, in your heart, I am different. I can be trusted. Tell me what you know so I can save my wife and bring her back to our child and me. Help me, I must save her before it's too late, and I will help you buy your freedom.

Do you swear to the gods that you will help?

You have my word. I swear on Tina, I will do whatever I can to set you free.

I believe you. My heart says I am to trust you. You are different.

Vesia, tell me everything. Anything you say may be necessary. Start from the beginning with that merchant Fapi.

Soon after I arrived, he started asking around the village about me. He learned that I was a house servant here. He seemed nice enough at first, and we soon became friends. He said he was interested in learning about what was happening at the villa. He offered me pieces of gold for any information I could tell him. It seemed harmless. I told him about the household's comings and goings. It seemed harmless, and soon I would have enough gold to buy my freedom.

What did you tell him?

It was just gossip, and who was here, when they left, where people were going—those types of things. I would never have gotten involved if I had known what they were planning. I would never have agreed to help if I had known they would kidnap my lady. Never. I am sorry. My hate blinded me. I thought they were after gold and jewelry. I should have known it was more. I should have known it would come to something as dreadful as this.

Vesia, now tell me about the night of the kidnapping. Where were you when it was happening?

I was already in my room when I heard the commotion. By the time I went to see, my lady was gone. They took her.

Vesia, you must be honest with me now if we are to help each other. Tell me everything you know. I need to know everything. What did you agree to do? What happened that night?

Fapi told me to distract the guard in the
south tower at midnight. I was to keep him
from noticing anyone who might approach
the villa. I told him no; this is not what I
agreed to do. I didn't want to get involved. He
said this time was different, and it would be
our last meeting. He handed me triple what
he usually paid. I had enough right there to
buy my freedom. So, I did it. I knew it was
wrong, but I couldn't go on another day living
the life of a slave. I had to do it. So, that night
I went to the south tower and kept the guard
occupied. I kept him very entertained. He
was not concerned with anything else that
might have been happening, only what was
right in front of him.

Did that merchant Fapi say anything about
the men breaking in?

No, just that they were here to rob my lady's
jewels. I never dreamed it was to kidnap her.
I am so sorry, Commander. I should have
known.

Nothing about them? Did he say where they
were from or where they were headed?

No, nothing, nothing like that. Oh wait, he
called them mercenaries. Good, did he
mention anything else? Where were they
from?

All he said about them was that they were
mercenaries and would be returning to
Corsica.

Corsica?

He said they were headed to Vulci to meet a merchant ship to return to Corsica. Fapi said he knew the ship, and it may still be there. He agreed to help me buy passage and be free.

Toscano, the King, has arrived. He's outside speaking with Matteo.

Your majesty, I am sorry I left so suddenly.

Given the circumstances, you are forgiven, Commander. Now, what have you learned?

My lord, the servant girl, Vesia, is a spy. She gave information about the villa to a merchant named Fapi. He told me it was King Altare who hired him. The King mercenaries to conduct the kidnapping. They're heading to Vulci to board a ship back to Corsica with Gia. I must leave at once if I am going to stop them.

Commander, rushing in alone will only get you killed. Take a company of my best guards and a decree of safe passage from me to King Vel Saties. It will be of great aid to you when you get there.

Thank you, your majesty, your decree is much appreciated, but a large group of guards will only slow me down.

I will join you, Toscano.

And I, Commander.

I am coming with you also.

Vera, you must stay here. I need you to take care of Donato. He must not be left without a family.

They have taken my sister, Toscano. You are not leaving here without me.

It'll be a dangerous undertaking, Vera. I am not sure what to expect.

She is my sister; I am going with you. I'll do whatever it takes to free her.

Commander, your son will be safe with me. There is no safer place for him in all of Etruria.

Thank you, my lord. We must leave now to make it to Vulci before dark.

CHAPTER 18: CORSICA

City of Vulci

Commander, the harbor is this way.

You there, which of these ships is leaving for Corsica?

Corsica? That ship is gone. It left with the afternoon tide hours ago.

What ship is heading out next?

See that two-masted merchant ship there. The last of their amphoras are being loaded now. It will be heading out on the morning tide.

Court of King Vel Saties

I need to see the King now. It is urgent.

That's not possible. He's retired for the evening. Come back in the morning.

I must not have been clear. I need to see your King now!

And I guess I didn't make myself clear, come back in the morning, and I'll see what I can do. Guards, show our guests, here, the way out.

Hold on, look at this. We're here on a decree from King Acri of Tressia. Bring this to your King. He knows who we are and will see us right away.

Commander, I would have hoped to see you back here under different circumstances. I am sorry to hear about such dreadful business. Tell me, how can I help you?

Your majesty, we believe the mercenaries who kidnapped my wife left Vulci on a trading vessel hours ago, heading for Corsica. A trading ship in the harbor is being loaded now that will set sail on the morning tide. Can you grant us passage to take it and intercept them?

You will not catch up to anyone on a loaded two-masted merchant ship. I will have a warship staffed and ready for you to leave by daybreak. With any luck, you will overtake that merchant ship before they reach port.

That's excellent, your majesty. You are most kind. I have one other favor I must ask of you, your majesty.

Of course, what else can I do?

One of your men, a soldier named Tarsus of Vacalvi, he may wish to join us. Do I have your permission to ask him?

You may. I know he and your general, Matteo, were close friends in their youth.

Yes, thank you, your majesty, and I am eternally grateful.

May the gods look favorably upon your mission, Commander.

The Port of Alalia on the Isle of Corsica

Look, Commander, an Etruscan merchant
ship is docked in the harbor. It looks like it's
still being unloaded. It must be the ship the
mercenaries used.

Are you the Captain?

It depends upon who's asking.

I'm asking, along with every member of that
warship over there.

What if I am?

Where were the mercenaries who were
aboard your ship?

What mercenaries? This is a merchant ship
transporting cargo, not mercenaries.

Listen, I am asking you again, politely, give
me the truth, or you'll be unloading the rest
of your precious cargo from the bottom of the
harbor. Now, where have they gone?

Hold on. I don't want any trouble. I'm only
interested in making a profit and not losing
my cargo. They paid me handsomely for their
passage and their privacy.

How handsomely?

They paid me ten coins each, plus five for the
slave.

Here's that, plus ten more. Now open your mouth. Where are they headed?

They didn't say, but I heard them talking about taking the slave to sell her to King Porsenna. That's all I know.

Tell me about this slave.

What about her? She looked like she would bring a high price. They kept her close, bound, gagged, and untouched.

How do I find this King Porsenna?

Just follow that wagon being loaded over there. They're taking that wine to the King. He bought my entire supply.

Here are another fifteen coins. Remain here 'till I get back. You'll get another fifteen for our passage back to Vulci when we return in the morning.

Be here before noon. The tides wait for no man, not even you, Commander.

Make room, my friend. You have passengers with an appointment with King Porsenna.

What's our plan, Commander? How do we free her? I've heard about this king; he's ruthless.

We will be using that to our advantage, Matteo.

City of Alalia

I'm Commander Toscano of the Army of
Tressia. Announce us now. We have urgent
business with the King.

Well, Commander Toscano, all the way from
Etruria. What brings you here to Alalia?

You, your majesty, I am interested in making
a deal with you for a recently acquired slave
in your possession.

I thought that might be the reason you are
here. But what possession do you have that
would be as interesting to me as this slave is
to you?

I hear you're a betting man, your majesty.
Your champion has made you a small fortune
over the years. Isn't that right, your majesty?

That he has, he is a true champion.

Well then, you must be willing to place a
wager on him. Your champion versus me. My
life for the freedom of that slave. I think you'd
enjoy that immensely.

You're right. I shall. It is done. You verse my
champion Turcius. Win, and the slave is
yours. Lose, and all your troubles are over.
What an unexpected pleasure. Good luck,
Commander, and may the victor enjoy his
spoils.

Commander, no, there must be another way.

This is the only way, Matteo. He won't remember me, but I have seen this Tarcius fight up close many times. He's a champion but has a weakness.

Fanum Voltumnae Fairgrounds, Fifteen Years Earlier

Where have you been, Toscano? Were you watching those boxers again? They'll be fighting again soon enough. We'll take some time and go to the arena together tomorrow and see them. But now I need you to get more wood for the fire. We still have plenty of weapons to produce while we're here. Now go, fetch me some more firewood. This flame is not hot enough.

The gladiators say your weapons are the finest blacksmith in Etruria, father.

It takes years to master this trade, Toscano. My father taught me, and I will teach you. But I can't do another thing until you get me more wood.

Here you are, father. My gods, look at this sword. You're an expert blacksmith, father. When did you know you wanted to be a blacksmith?

It was soon after I first started as an apprentice with my father. I was amazed at seeing him working that ore, magically turning it into weapons of bronze. His workmanship was outstanding, and he had the most beautiful weapons I had ever seen. It is a skill only very few can master. He taught well during those first years. But he also made sure I learned from others. He sent me to also apprentice with other blacksmiths until he thought I had learned all there was to know about our craft. With his advice, I soon produced fine bronze weapons and armor. That is when I knew this was what I wanted to do for the rest of my life. It will be the same for you, Toscano. When you start producing quality weapons, you'll find your desire. Toscano, someday you will be known as the finest blacksmith in Etruria.

How old were you when you knew this, father?

I was not that much older than you are now. But let's go to sleep now. We'll speak more about this tomorrow. It's late now, and we need our rest. We have much to do tomorrow before I can take you back to the stadium.

Good night, father.

Good night, my son.

Fanum Voltumnae Stadium

Your son, there, Toscano, how old is he?

He'll be thirteen in a month.

160

He has considerable size and strength for his age. He has the balance and instincts of a natural fighter.

He has other skills as well.

Have you considered him for the arena? With his talent, I can mold him into a grand champion.

That is not his destiny. He is to follow in his father's trade.

Are you sure of that, smithy?

Did you see that father? I saw him do that in training. That's his best move. Tarcius is going to win again, I'm sure. He's the best by far and will be a famous champion one day. You'll see.

Toscano, it's time we leave.

Can we stay a little longer, father? We have yet to see the boxers.

Come, we must go. It is already late. We must go back and start to pack.

Fanum Voltumnae Fairgrounds

Toscano, pick up those last few shields and that helmet over there. I'll be right back with the wagon.

Wait, father, we need to talk.

What about? It is time we leave; we have a long journey ahead of us. We'll have plenty of time to talk on our way back home.

No, father, please, we need to talk now.

What is so urgent, Toscano?

I don't want to leave, father.

What are you talking about, Toscano? The festival is over. We'll be back next season, I promise you.

I want to stay here, father. The trainer, Cutu, has offered me an apprenticeship. He has trained the best wrestlers and boxers in all of Etruria. He wants to talk to you.

Toscano, that's no life for you. You're going to be a great blacksmith. I will train you; the arena is no place for you. It's a dangerous life.

Father, blacksmithing is your life and your dream for me. It is not mine. Father, the arena, I feel it. That is what I must do. It's where I want to be, father. You are happy following your dreams, Father. Allow me to follow mine.

Toscano, I can't just leave you here. We need to return home, and I can't go without you. You are too young to decide on this now. Too young for any of this. We'll talk on the journey home. Now it's time to leave, come, come home with me. Now is not the time to talk about all of this.

Father, I love you, but you must let me do this. You must let me, father. I know this is what I want to do. If you force me to go back home, I will only leave and come right back here.

I'll be back home after my training is done in a few months. There are several here at the school already and younger than I am. Let me join them, father. I've been practicing with them since we've been here. Cutu runs the finest gladiator school in all of Etruria. When the training is done, he promises to pass by Tressia on his way to Pisa. Father, please let me stay and train here. It's what I need to do.

Training Grounds Outside Fanum Voltumnae Stadium

Your boy has the raw talent and spirit of a true champion. Those things cannot be taught.

Cutu, I will find you if any harm comes to him.

Lucien, Lucien, my friend, he'll be treated well, as if he was my son. He'll learn excellent skills here at the school that will serve him well for his entire life. You have my word, Lucien. He'll come back to you a man in the fall.

Now, listen, Toscano, if you are not happy here, if you are not treated right, and if anything is not suitable, you are to leave at once and return to us.

Father, don't worry. I am old enough to know what I'm doing. This school is right for me, father. I already have many friends. This is what I must do. I will take care of myself, I promise you. Now go, father, please. I will be back home in three months. I love you, father.

I'm proud of you, son. I will miss you.

CHAPTER 19: THE BATTLE OF ALALIA

The Arena in the City of Alalia

Tarsus, our trainer, Cutu, sends his regards.

What?

Surely you remember him, our trainer, Cutu.
And me, do I look at all familiar?

You? How do I know you?

Look at me closely. My name is Toscano.
Toscano of Tressia.

Are you the blacksmith's son? Little Toscano?

Yes, it's me, Tarsus. But I'm no longer that
young boy who sparred with you back then. I
see you still fight with those same moves he
taught you. He was my teacher too, Cutu, for
a long while. I learned well after you left. I
learned how to defeat a much larger person
than myself. Shall I show you, Tarcius?

Do what you must. We'll soon see who the
better student was.

Yes, we will.

Kill him! Kill him! Kill him!

Shall we save your champion live to fight
another day, your majesty? Or are you done
with him and ready for the new Champion of
Alalia to take his place? What do you say,
your majesty? His life is in the hands of his
King; live or die?

Let him live. He needs to earn back the coin
he lost for me today.

And are you to be true to your word, your
majesty, and will now set her free?

I am a man of my word. To the victor belongs
his spoils. Aguilo, bring me his winnings.
Toscano, now you must join me to celebrate
your great victory.

Thank you, your majesty. You are a man true
to your word, but we must leave. Our vessel
awaits our return.

Your majesty, you're letting them go?

For now. Aguilo. But take a dozen men and
follow them. When they bed down for the
night, kill them all and bring me back the
head of Toscano. He deserves a place of
honor in our arena, a true champion.

Campsite in the Hills Outside the City of Alalia

Gia!

Toscano, you have saved me, my gods, my
love. I can't believe you are here.

You are safe now. You are back with me. No
one will ever take me away from you again.

Oh, Toscano.

I could not rest until you were back in my
arms. I love Toscano.

We must keep going. We must get far away
from this place before it's too late. This king
will not rest until he has his revenge.

Matteo, we make camp here for the night;
this is the perfect spot to set camp. It is only a
few hours further to the harbor. Set the
campfire there, out away from the hillside.

Commander, a campfire? Do you think that is
wise? It'll give our position away for miles if
we are being followed.

That is precisely my intention. Nico, Tarsus,
come close. I have a plan. Take off your
cloaks, fill them with bushes and twigs, and
lay them up around the campfire. I want it to
seem like we are all bedded there for the
night. We'll conceal ourselves here, along the
hillside. We'll move in and strike them from
behind after they pass.

Well devised, Commander.

Gia, Vera, knowing this king, he's not going
just to let us go. He has likely sent a group to
ambush us. They must be close by us by now,
having seen our fire. They will wait to
ambush us until we're bedded down for the
night. Listen to this plan. That campfire, set
there, is a decoy. We'll stay here, hidden out
of sight behind these boulders. We'll let them
pass us. When they enter the camp, we attack
them from behind. I want you two to remain
concealed here. Take these weapons just in
case we're discovered. Do what you must and
then make a run for it. Are you two clear?

Do not worry about us, Tuscano. We'll be fine.

How many do you think there will be, Commander?

Thall be ten at most, Nico, and be completely shocked when we strike them from behind. It will be over quickly. The key will be having them pass by us unnoticed. So, we move back here, conceal yourselves well, and remain still until we attack on my signal.

Commander Aguilo, they've bedded down for the night.

Follow me, men. No one is to be taken alive.

Commander, listen. I can hear them approaching.

They're here.

Be still and let them pass. Now, you two remain here. Get ready, men; slowly, follow me. No one must get away.

Look, Commander, there, those two, they're getting away.

I have them.

I see you haven't lost your aim, Matteo.

You keep me in good practice, Commander.

Vera, I thought I told you to stay back.

168

I always had trouble obeying orders. Gia can attest to that.

Where did you learn to throw a dagger like that?

Matteo has been teaching me; we've been practicing.

She's a fast learner, Commander. And can split a pear in half at twenty paces.

I can see that. Let's hope she never gets mad at either one of us.

Are you all right, Gia?

I'm fine. Vera, as usual, wouldn't listen. She wouldn't stay behind. She never listens.

I know. Well, at least this time, I'm glad she didn't.

There's so much blood here. Let's move now. We could make it to the port before daybreak and get sleep aboard the ship before we set sail.

Commander, you're early.

We seemed to have overstayed our welcome with this king. When do we set sail, Captain?

We can leave within the hour now that you're here.

Good, I don't want to be here when any surprise guests might arrive.

The Tyrrhenian Sea off the coast of Corsica

Captain, how long before we reach Vulci?

The wind is favorable, and the crew is keeping pace. If this keeps up, we should be in Vulci before evening.

Captain, look behind us.

It looks like a patrol ship, a Greek Trireme.

It's coming on us fast, Captain.

Double speed!

Do you think we can outrun her?

It's possible; we're not fully unloaded and have a rested crew. I'll know for sure within the next five minutes.

It is still gaining, Captain. And it's not just a single patrol ship. There are at least eight more sails in the distance behind her.

We head towards the coast. If we are lucky, we'll make it to the river Golo before they reach us. They'll lose some ground, and there are many streams that we can hide in along the way up the river.

Captain, they're closing fast.

Why are they all so interested in us? It doesn't make any sense.

Captain, off the starboard bow, sails as far as you can see; Captain, warships, they look Etruscan.

It looks like the entire Etruscan fleet. Now, this is going to be interesting.

What do you think is going on, Captain?

It looks like we have ended up in the middle of what could be the largest naval battle I've ever seen.

Captain, the Trireme is changing course. It looks like they're maneuvering to circle the Etruscan fleet.

Are you sure?

I have seen it before, Captain. I've served in the Vulcian navy for two years.

Tarsus? You have?

Yes, I transferred to the navy soon after I arrived in Vulci. It was either that or the copper mines in the hills of Tolfa, and I found out quickly that the sea was a much better option than those mineshafts.

The Talfa Hills, Years Earlier

Tarsus, hand me that lamp. Look at this. It's another vein, and it's starting right here. It leads straight up. I'm going to follow it. You keep digging where you are.

171

Marcel, I'm going back up. My basket is full.
I'll join you at that vein when I return.

What's that?

It's a collapse, a big one.

Marcel, he's down there. He could be trapped.
We must find him.

This whole shaft has collapsed, Tarsus.
There's no way we can reach him.

We must! We must start digging! We must
reach him!

If he was in this shaft, Tarsus, he's gone,
crushed to death. Do you understand me,
Tarsus? We must get out now. He's dead. This
whole gallery is about to come down. Taurus,
he's dead, now come on, get out. Now!
Tarsus! Now! Before it's too late for us.

I'm never going down a mine shaft again,
Sethra. I can't, not after today. I just can't.

Well, you can petition for a transfer. How do
you feel about the sea?

What? Me? Join the navy?

They are always looking for more crew.

What do you know about the navy?

You will have a better chance of staying alive
at sea than working in these mines here.

I have never even been aboard a ship. I can't even swim.

Swim? If you are thrown into the sea, it's best not to swim. It's better to resign yourself to your fate and drown peacefully.

Have you been aboard a ship?

A long time ago, when I first came of age.

What was it like?

You break your back from dawn to dusk, strapped to an oar. You then eat and sleep, and the next day you wake and do it all over again. It goes on day after day until you are rammed, sunk in a storm, or reach a port.

It sounds worse than this.

It's not that bad. If you are lucky, you move to an upper deck. There you'll breathe the fresh sea air, eat well, and retire well if you live long enough.

The Tyrrhenian Sea off the coast of Corsica

Captain, we'll be overtaken before we reach the river.

Do you have a better idea, Tarsus?

Yes, head back out to sea towards the Etruscan navy.

And get mixed up in the battle, in a merchant ship? We won't last long. And what do you think we can do? Attack a Trireme?

Yes, we'll have a chance with what I have in mind.

Against a Trireme?

We won't be ramming. We disable her broadside and let the Etruscan navy finish her off.

How do you intend to do that? She's triple our size, with dozens on board and twice our speed.

That's all true, but we have some advantages.

Like what?

We are much more maneuverable and have one feature they lack.

What feature?

Our oars they're not fixed, and we can ship them quickly. The Greeks have their oars attached at the pivot and can't be released quickly.

How would that help us?

We quickly turn at the Trireme when it gets within range and run at her broadside, crushing her oars before they can be retracted. She will be left almost motionless in the water for a long while.

174

Broadsiding a Trireme? With a merchant ship?

They'll be unprepared, Captain, with no idea what we are up to until we are right on them. We'll take cover as we pass. They won't be able to board us from the side. If we're lucky, it will leave them disabled in the water long enough for us to escape. It will take time for them to transfer enough oars and men to get moving again.

Interesting, Tarsus, it could work. It will take timing and fast maneuvering, but it could work. I'm sure we'll take a lashing as we pass, but we should be long gone before they can move again.

Toscano, what do you think?

Tarsus, have you done this before?

With a merchant ship? No, no one would be that foolish. But I have seen Triremes broadsided with their oars being crushed and lying disabled in battle.

If you don't have another idea, I think it's our best choice, Captain.

Men, listen, I'll have the Trireme come up on our starboard side. I'll give the order to come about when she's fifty paces a stern. We'll turn, heading straight towards her broadside. Right before we reach her, I will give the order for portside to ship oars, and we'll ram right up her broadside, crushing her oars as we pass.

Tuscano, have your men ready on the bow. They will not be expecting this, so you should have plenty of targets for your arrows.

We'll be ready. Gia, Vera, take cover below deck. I will let you know when it is safe to come back up.

Gia, now, go quickly.

Tuscano, I love you. May the gods protect us.

Ready men, she's about where we want her.

The maneuver was timed perfectly. We quickly swung about, facing right down on the Trireme within seconds. Our port oars were pulled before we broadsided her, and the ship jolted as the two hulls smashed against each other. As we scraped by, you could hear their oars splitting in two and screaming from the men below deck being jolted forward, still lashed to their oars. Our rigging and sails were ripped apart as we scraped beneath their overhanging decking. Soon a barrage of arrows and javelins came raining down on us. But with our sails torn and strewn all over the deck, they couldn't accurately strike at us.

Grappling irons came raining down, thrown as we passed. They tumbled across our deck. One latched onto our port side gunnel, and the ship jolted hard as the barbs grabbed hold, penetrating deep into the wood. We were trapped.

Toscano, what are you doing? Where are you going?

To release us.

You can't reach the end of the chain. Don't climb out there. You'll end up in the sea. Toscano! Stop!

Man overboard!

Quickly throw him a line! Toscano! Toscano!

Captain, we're freed.

Where is he? Toscano! Toscano, where are you? We must go back! We've got to find him!

With these seas, there's nothing we can do; we'll never find him

Turn us around, Captain. Now! Or you'll be joining him. Now! Captain!

We can't turn back that Trireme will ram us.

I said turn us around, or I'll slit your throat right here, from ear to ear.

Matteo, he's here somewhere; we must find him!

Toscano! Toscano! Please, Toscano, where are you?

Gia, it's getting dark. We can't circle much longer.

We can't go. We must find him. I won't leave without him.

177

There's nothing more we can do. It's too dark now to see anything in the water. I'm so sorry, Gia, we must go.

Matteo, I can't leave him. We must keep looking. Matteo, Nico, please, we must keep looking.

Gia, I'm sorry, he's gone. We must go while we still can.

Vera, it's Toscano. We must save him!

I know, I know. I'm so sorry, Gia. I'm so sorry.

CHAPTER 20: THE IRON COAST

Somewhere on the Tyrrhenian Sea

I pushed my way back up to the surface, gulping for a breath as my face cleared the water. Spinning around, I could see both ships sailing away from me. The sea was in turmoil, waves coming from all directions, crashing over me every few seconds. It was difficult just to breathe. My clothes weighed me down, making it difficult to swim or even move. I tore open my tunic, hoping it would help me move freely in the water. But wave after wave continued to pound me, and I struggled to keep my head above water. I was becoming utterly disorientated, tossed repeatedly by the towering waves.

My eyes started to burn from the continual drenching in the salty water, and now I could barely see. As I rose to the top of one wave, I saw part of an oar jutting up out of another twenty paces in front of me. Summing all my strength, I swam towards it. But it drifted away from me even faster.

For the first time, I started to think I would not survive. I was going to drown. I took a few more strokes, but it was hopeless. My strength and determination were gone. I was barely able to breathe. I thought of giving in to the sea and wondered what would happen if I stopped struggling and let myself sink. How would it feel to drown? What would happen next if I let my body slip beneath the surface? I began to think of Gia and saw her reaching out for me, calling, "Toscano, come, come back to me; you must come back to me." She gave me the strength to continue.

But as the hours passed, my body began to feel heavier and heavier. My arms and legs were so weak that I could not move them. I became so cold that my body started to shiver, and I struggled to keep my head above the water. I had no strength left to continue. I was gasping for my last breath. It was time to make peace with the gods and tell Gia that I loved her and would see her again in heaven.

I closed my eyes, letting my body go limp, and quickly slipped below the surface. The further I sank, the colder, darker, and more silent it became. I felt at peace as I descended deeper into the sea, ready to release my last breath and allow the water to rush into my lungs. Then I heard a voice. It was my father.

"Toscano, you must live. You must swim, Toscano, as I taught you." I felt a rush of energy, and my arms and legs began to move without thinking. I started to move, and I heard his voice even louder, "reach Toscano, reach, reach up." I gave a strong kick, extended my arm with my fingers fully outstretched, and touched something. I kicked again and reached out to grab it. It was solid; it was the oar. I pulled it towards me with all my strength and erupted out of the water, gasping for air. I'm alive!

Catching my breath, I wrapped my arms tightly over my oar, clinking to it as firmly as possible, amazed to be alive and gently floating on the surface.

Fortunately, the piece of oar I grabbed was large enough to keep me comfortably afloat. I

could see the splintered end where it had
snapped in two against the ship's hull poking
out of the water. I steady myself on the oar
by pressing my cheek on top of it. I had to
kick to balance myself, and I slowly began to
move forward.

It was now completely dark, but finally, the
winds had calmed, and the waves no longer
broke on top of me. I somehow found the
strength to continue kicking this way for
hours. At one point, I tried wrapping my legs
over the oar to relieve the pressure on my
arms, but it was too slippery, and I spun over
it, ending up underwater. I had no choice but
to put it back under my arms, pull it tightly
against my chest and resume kicking.

After hours, my arms became completely
numb, and I lost my grip on the oar. I raised
my head over the top and used the bottom of
my chin to help me cling on. It worked for a
while, relieving my arms, but my neck soon
grew tired, and I went back, clinging tightly
only with my arms.

Huge swells began to emerge, carrying me up
and forward, then rolling away beneath me.
The motion was soothing. I had to fight to
keep awake and maintain my grip on my
lifesaving oar. The night sky began to clear
and filled with thousands of stars. Off to my
right, I spotted the North Star. It remained
motionless as the rest of the stars seemed to
rotate around it. I thought keeping it to my

right would guide me back to the Corsican coast.

I rolled smoothly among the waves throughout the night, fighting to stay awake. My mind began to drift back to my childhood. I remembered the first time I had seen the sea. My father took me to my first spring festival at Fanum Voltumnae. I must have been about six. Traveling there, one bend in the road opened close to a broad bay. I asked my father what it was. He smiled as he looked at me and said, "let's go and find out." He stopped the cart near the water's edge, and I quickly jumped out. As we walked in the sand, my father held his hand as we headed for the sea. I can still feel his long, calloused fingers gripping mine. We took off our sandals as we neared the water's edge and ran barefoot through the warm wet sand into the cool, clear blue water.

Looking down at my feet, I could see a school of small fish all darting away in different directions, frightened by our shadows. I remember reaching down into the water to pick up a bright, cone-shaped seashell resting near my feet. I showed it to my father, and his words have stayed with me to this day, "You found a treasure. The world is full of treasures. You must reach out and grab them before they pass you by."

I also remember seeing other children swimming and laughing off in the distance. My father looked at me and said, "I guess it's time for you to learn to swim." He let go of my hand and said, "go ahead and try." I looked back down at the water and made myself fall forward, headfirst, straight in. It felt amazing, sinking below the surface, surrounded by water for the first time. As I dropped deeper, I tried to breathe, but I swallowed a mouth full of water instead and began to choke.

Right then, my eyes sprung open, and I realized I was dreaming. Looking up at the sky, I thought it must have been for a while because I could now see it was almost dawn. Ahead, I could see a line of clouds just above the horizon; staring at them; their outline grew stronger. Wait, those aren't clouds; they're mountains, catching the sunrise. It's a coastline. I've made it to shore! I'm going to survive!

I began to kick urgently now, and with the help of the following tide, I was headed right toward them. Soon a bay was forming into view, with a crescent beach appearing at the shore. I began to kick even faster, pushing the oar ahead of me. I now heard the waves crashing on the beach. I decided to abandon my lifesaving oar and swim freestyle the last hundred yards to the beach.

As I drew closer, I reached for the bottom, and after a few tries, I could finally feel my sandals touching the ground. I took a few more strokes and tried to stand, but a wave knocked me back into the water. I didn't care. I closed my eyes, happy to lay there, half on the shore and half my body still in the water. I lay there for a while, simply glad to be alive. I eventually opened my eyes, and there, resting on the sand next to me, was a bright white, cone-shaped seashell. The same treasure I saw years ago with my father. I reached and grabbed it. It was my reward, a gift from him, and a reminder that he saved my life.

I rose and slowly began to walk up the beach. But after a few steps, I had to sit. I didn't have the energy to move much further. I could see rock outcroppings bordered the beach on both sides. I looked inland and studied the mountainside ahead of me. The foothills were thick with trees. But staring at them, I could see one area with a cherry tree grove.

Inspired, I found the energy to return and head toward them. The air was full of the cherry blossom scent as I drew near. My timing was perfect. The trees were loaded with deep red, ripened cherries. Reaching up, I pulled down a branch and grabbed a handful of the sweetest cherries I had ever

184

tasted. By the time I was full, my fingers, lips, and teeth had all been dyed a deep red. I sat satisfied against one of the trees, resting comfortably until my strength was fully restored.

It was now close to dark, and I had to figure out where I was. I went down to the beach to get an unobstructed view of the area. And off in the distance, I could see a column of smoke rising above the tree line. I found my new heading.

My clothes were starting to dry, and salt was caking up everywhere on me, especially in my hair. I needed to wash and clean up. The caking salt was getting more unbearable with every step. Grateful ahead, I could see a small stream running out to the sea. I stepped right in, stopping in the middle of the stream and diving in, letting the cool, clear water rush over me.

Refreshed, I continued my journey. I slowed when I heard the clanging of metal coming from a short distance ahead of me. Moving up closer, I could see the origins of the fire. A bright orange flame shot out of a well-built furnace, revealing the three men working there.

From its size and other buildings off in the distance, it was becoming clear that this was a sizable mining camp and smelting operation. I tried to hear what they were saying, but I couldn't distinguish anything from where I was hidden. I moved in a bit closer. I could see the ore now. It looked different. It wasn't the green, dull copper ore or the thin translucent crystals of tin. This ore had shiny, bright yellow metallic particles reflecting in the flame. As the ore's rock was heated, I could see the metal dripping to the bottom of the furnace. One of the men used a bellows to force air into the soft, malleable red mass, turning it bright yellow, while another worker pulled out some and repeatedly beat and folded it.

I had never seen my father work like this. This was not copper or even bronze they were working on; it was much different. My father spoke of a new metal being smelted in Sparta; he called it iron. When performed correctly, the swords produced were rigid, with a sharp, long-lasting edge, making them one of the most valuable weapons on earth. It was one of the reasons the Spartan army was so feared. I now realize that I had stumbled upon the first iron-producing mine in Etruria.

I circled the camp moving close to a building two workers had just entered. I could hear them speaking. They were talking about finishing the load in the morning, carting it off to the shore, ready to be picked up, and heading for Tarchina. I decided to show myself, and I walked out to the clearing. I heard ferocious growling and spotted a dog charging right toward me. I was in trouble. As he lunged at my throat, I raised my arm just in time. He tore at my arm, knocking me down. Without thinking, I pulled out my

dagger and stuck it into his stomach. He fell
to the side with a whimper, taking me with
him. I rose to my feet but before I could take
a step, the tip of a sword pressed against my
back.

Drop the dagger and put your hands out
where I can see them. Tell me who you are
and why you're sneaking around here, the
truth, or I'll feed you to that furnace.

I don't mean any harm. My name is Toscano
of Tressia. I washed up on a beach near here
and saw your fire.

Were you shipwrecked?

No, I was aboard a merchant ship that set sail
from Alalia, and we found ourselves being
pursued by a Greek Trireme patrolling off the
coast. We tried to outrun her, but it kept
closing, and our only escape was to turn and
broadside her.

In a merchant's vessel, are you broadsiding a
Trireme?

I know it sounds foolish, but it worked. We
disabled her and were getting away until
they managed to grapple us.

So, the ship was captured, and you were
thrown overboard?

No, I was tossed into the sea when I tried to
cut the line holding us.

And you freed the ship and swam all the way here?

More like drifting here. I was able to grab hold of a shattered oar to stay afloat.

You're not on the coast of Corsica, far from it. You're on the island of Elba.

Elba? The currents must be stronger than I realized.

That's quite a tale. It doesn't explain why you were spying on us, even if I believe it.

I thought I was back in Corsica, and it's not known to be too welcoming to Etruscans, so I wanted to know what I was getting into before I showed myself. I am happy to be alive and back on Etruscan soil. I'm sorry for what happened to your dog. I will repay you.

This merchant ship you say you were on, what's its name?

Bonitas, and her captain is Sivas, Captain Sivas.

The Bonitas, out of Vulci, exactly how did you end up on her?

We bought a passage for the trip back to Vulci.

We?

I was traveling with my wife and her sister, heading back home to Tressia from Corsica.

188

Corsica is a long way from Tressia and not where you would typically take a wife. What were you doing there? And what is it that you do? Are you a merchant of some kind?

Why all these questions? I would just like your help to get back to the mainland. Can I ask you a question? What is being mined here?

That is not your concern. Sapu, bring me some cord. I want to tie him up tight. We don't want to have him running off.

Supa, show our guest his accommodation here in that storage shed. Be sure he's tied down well. We'll have him stew for a while. He has more to tell us.

Do you think he knows we are smelting iron?

There is more to his story; he knows more than he lets on. At dawn, I want you and Blasius to take the fishing boat back to Piombino and head down to Vulci. Pass around some coins and learn as much as possible about our shipwrecked hostage and his tale. I need to know if he is telling the truth. And Supa, get back here as soon as you can.

Campo Nell'elba

I awoke the following day to a bucket of water thrown in my face.

Now, the truth, if you want to leave here alive. Start talking.

I am telling you the truth. I washed up here and stumbled upon your camp. I don't particularly care what you are doing here. I am only interested in getting back to Tressia. You will be paid handsomely for your trouble if you help me to secure passage to the mainland. What did you say your name is?

I didn't say.

Fine, let's start over. Release me, and we can help each other. I have several friends close to Vulci. They would be incredibly grateful to you if you aid me now.

Like whom?

The King, for one.

Why would you know the King of Vulci?

There is much about me you do not know. Set me free, and you'll be rewarded.

Tell me more about yourself before I decide what I will do with you.

As I already told you, my name is Toscano. I was in Corsica to free my wife. She was kidnapped, and I followed her there to free her. We were attacked on our return, and I was tossed overboard, freeing our ship. That is all the truth. Now, will you help me?

This is all very impressive. We'll talk more. For now, I need to get back to work.

Wait, untie me! Let me out! I am telling you the truth.

We'll see about that.

I needed to get out of this place, but first, I wanted to be sure what was being smelted. If it is iron, it could change the balance of power in the entire region.

I rubbed the cord, binding my hands up and down along the edge of the stake, securing me to the ground. It finally started to fray enough that it ripped apart, and I could free my hands. I then untied my feet and looked for a way out. The front door was barricaded from the outside. But looking at the base next to it, I could see that it had settled a bit, and a few of the mud bricks along the bottom rows had cracked and loosened from the motor holding them in place. A good back kick might jar them loose.

I could hear the constant tamping from the furnace as the men worked the metal bloom. I decided to try to time my kick with the strike of the metal to muffle the sound. On my third strike, the bricks loosened enough that I could remove them. Clearing away the debris, I had created enough space to crawl out.

But before I made a bolt for the woods, I could see an outline of twenty to thirty amphoras stacked along the rear wall of the shed. That was a lot for a mining camp of this size. I went to take a closer look. As I suspected, they were not filled with wine or olive oil. I dragged it over into the light near the doorway and looked inside. Oddly, it was filled with sand. And when I reached into the sand, I felt something solid, and then another. They were bars of iron hidden throughout the amphora. I dragged it back with the others and dashed for the opening I had just created.

Atticus! He's gone!

Quickly follow me. He's heading for the water.

Village of Cavo, On the Island Elba

I knew I would be spotted if I headed directly to the beach, so I traveled inland along the coast, hoping to come across a harbor or small fishing village. Through the clearings, I could see that the straits had narrowed enough now to see the opposite shore. It wasn't long before I came across a small cove with a dozen fishing boats pulled up on the beach. I slid down the cliff towards the first boat I saw, pushed it into the water, and shoved it off. I was finally on my way home. It took 'till dawn to row across the straits but outlined in the moonlight, I could see the coastal town of Piombino up on the bluff.

192

After beaching the boat, I climbed up the bank and made my way inland. It was dawn when I reached the road to Vulci. It would take me at least two days traveling by foot to get there. A passing wagon might take me at least part of the way if I got lucky.

Campo Nell'elba

Atticus, his story is true. He is the commander of the Tressian army. I was told that his wife was kidnapped and sold into slavery in Corsica. I spoke to one of the warship crew that took them to Corsica. He was able to free her and got away on the Bonitas. But soon after they left the harbor, a Greek Trireme spotted them. In a daring move, they broadsided her, and he was thrown into the sea.

He got away on the Bonitas. Well, that's incredible, but it does us no good now. He managed to escape and had already left the island. Sapu, this whole encounter stays with us. If King Altera were ever to discover that we had his enemy's commander captive and let him escape, he'd have us killed, no matter how much iron we supplied him. Do you understand? Not a word to anyone. We never met that man.

Court of King Vel Saties of Vulci

Toscano, I was told you were lost at sea. It's hard to believe you are alive.

The gods were with me, your majesty. Can you tell me what happened with the naval battle with the Greeks?

Our losses were significant, but so were theirs. They eventually retreated, and we have taken all of Corsica.

Praise to the gods! Your majesty, I have vital information to share with you also.

Yes, go ahead.

The merchant ship Bonitas, do you know she travels to Elba on her route?

I do. Her captain trades with us for the tin, copper, silver, and flint mined there.

Something else is mined there, a metal more valuable than tin or copper, and is being smuggled out and delivered to King Altare.

By Captain Sivas?

Yes, he carries it hidden in the amphoras on his trading route.

What is this metal?

It is iron, your majesty.

If iron is being mined on Elba and in the hands of King Altare, it is perilous for us all.

If his ship is still in port, you could recover what he has hidden and see it yourself.

Thank you for telling me, Toscano. I will find Captain Silvas and find the underlying cause of this. You must be eager to return home to your wife, and I will no longer detain you. Your king will also be anxious to hear this news about the iron being mined on Elba. Please let him know I am eager to meet with him. Now, you must go. I will have my guards and a messenger ride with you. May the gods continue looking favorably upon you, Toscano.

Thank you, your majesty.

Private Chambers of King Vel Saties of Vulci

He must never reach Tressia. Do you understand, Sethra?

Yes, my lord, it will be done.

The Lemon Forrest

Sethra, why are we stopping here? We can make it to Tressia before nightfall if we hurry.

It will be just for a moment. The horses need to drink.

Looking at their faces when we stopped, I realized what this escort was all about. I took my chance and bolted away as fast as I could.

Stop him, you fool. Quick, after him! Don't let him get away!

I was in a full gallop for a short distance when the path turned and narrowed. I ducked a bit and grabbed hold of an overhanging branch. I pulled it back as far as I could. Then letting it go, it snapped back right into the face of the first rider after me, flinging him off his horse and landing hard on the ground. He fell backward from his horse, smashing his head on a rock.

The others continued, barely pausing to look back at him. The second rider was able to catch up alongside me. He leaped off his horse at me, and we both tumbled to the ground. Struggling, he lunged at me with his dagger. My years of training took over. Bending back his wrist, I forced the blade out of his hand and reached over to grab it. I swung my legs over his shoulders and pinned him to the ground. With one hand, I pushed his face into the ground and, with the other, slit his throat.

As I rose, I turned and saw the third charging me with his horse. I darted to the side, pulled him off to the ground, jumped onto his horse, and rode off. Two riders remained. The path turned again, running alongside a ravine. Looking ahead, I could see it was narrowing, and a well-timed jump could clear the other side. I turned towards it, gave my horse a swift kick, and we raced towards the edge. At the last second, we leaped and landed safely on the other side. Both riders following me stopped for a moment and turned back. I thought it was over for a moment, but one turned back towards me and went into a full gallop. His horse leaped, but it was too early. His forelegs reached the other side, but his hind legs hit the bank. The horse stumbled backward, and he fell off, careening down the ravine. His horse landed on top of him, crushing him to death.

Sethra was the last rider. Seeing the fall, he circled farther back to start his run. He timed the jump perfectly and made it safely across. The chase continued. We galloped for a distance before he could gain enough ground to come alongside me. I reached over and grabbed his tunic, yanking him off his horse. He tumbled between us, landing under his horse. I looked back and saw him lying motionless, trampled by his horse.

CHAPTER 21: THE COMING OF STEEL

Villa Feonia

My lady, a horse is approaching.

Go, see who it is.

Can it be? Commander? My gods, it's him.
He's alive. My lady! Come quick! My lady! It is
him! It's the Commander! He's alive!

Oh, my gods! It is you! You are alive! My love!
Toscano! My Toscano!

Gia! I made it back to you!

Toscano! Oh, my gods! I cannot believe my
eyes! The gods have given you back to me!
We're together again. I have you back! I'm

not letting you go! I prayed for them to save you, Toscano, and now they have answered my prayers.

Your prayers did save me, Gia. They gave me the strength to make it back to you.

Toscano, we searched and searched and never found you. I didn't want to leave, Toscano. They were telling me you drowned. I'm never letting you go. I can't breathe without you.

Gia, it's I who cannot breathe now. Loosen your hug, or this may be a short reunion.

Vera! Come quick! It's Toscano! He is alive!

Toscano? My gods, a spirit walks among us! I cannot believe my eyes. It is you!

It is me in the flesh. It's so good to see you, Vera. Now, where is my son? Bring him to me, please. He needs to see his father, and his father needs to see him!

Gia, I must ask you something. Something I couldn't stop thinking about while I was struggling to stay alive.

Yes, anything, Toscano.

Gia, will you marry me?

Toscano, what do you mean to marry you? We are already married. You took my hand in front of my sister and your family.

I mean for us to be formally married, in a wedding, here at the villa. You were in my thoughts endlessly. Our love kept me going. I promised myself we would have a formal ceremony if I were to make it back to you. Gia, will you marry me again?

Oh yes, my love, yes, I will marry you all over again.

May I have your left hand?

Oh, my gods.

With this band, I pledge my love to you and our marriage engagement.

It is so beautiful, Toscano. I love you dearly.

Now all that is left is choosing a date and having our proper wedding.

Vera, come quick, there's going to be a wedding. Here look, look at this ring. Toscano and I are going to have a wedding here at the villa.

Gia, how wonderful. When? When do you think it will be?

I'm too excited to think now, but soon, very soon.

Court of King Acri

Commander, it is good to see you alive. I received word that you were lost at sea, escaping from a Greek Trireme. It's good to know you're a naval commander, as well.

I'm afraid my skills at sea have more to do with floating than battling, your majesty.

Well, I am thrilled you survived.

Your majesty, I learned some interesting information we need to discuss.

Of course, continue.

Your majesty, I washed ashore on the island of Elba and soon stumbled upon a mining camp operating there. The camp was smelting a metal undiscovered here. Iron, your majesty.

Iron? On Elba?

Yes, your majesty. And there's more. I have never seen the process before, but it is being smelted there.

That is incredible, right here on Elba. Iron in King Mastarna of Vetulonia's hands could be a significant disadvantage.

I don't believe the king knows that iron is being smuggled off the island.

How is that so?

I found bars hidden in the sand inside the amphoras to be loaded onto a merchant ship.

Do you know the name of this ship?

The Bonitas, sailing out of Vulci. Its captain is Sivas, Captain Sivas. I heard them say it was heading for Tarchina to be sold to King Altare.

Who else knows about this?

I spoke about this King Vel Saties. He is not the ally we have come to expect.

What are you saying, Toscano?

Once I told the king what I had learned about the iron, he wished me safe travels and arranged for me to kill on the journey.

King Vel Saties?

Yes, your majesty. He had his riders escort me, and shortly after we were on our way, they attacked and intended to kill me.

Toscano, do you know what this means?

I do, your majesty. King Altare has bought our ally, and now our enemies have conspired to gain a significant military advantage. It must not be left unchecked.

Exactly. How long do you estimate this mining operation on Elba has been going on?

It is hard for me to say, your majesty, but from the appearance of the furnaces, I would estimate over two years.

They could have mined a substantial amount of iron during that time and may already have had an arsenal of iron weapons for their armies. We must act quickly. Be ready to leave for Vetulonia tomorrow and take a

message to King Mastarna. I will explain
more about your mission before you go.

Tressia Barracks

Matteo, Nico, on the king's orders, we are
taking a trip to Vetulonia, be ready to leave at
dawn.

Villa Feonia

Are you leaving so soon?

Gia, it will not be for long. It is for a mission
for the king. I will be back soon. A few weeks
at most. We will plan our wedding and pick a
date when I get back. I promise you.

Court of King Mastarna

Your majesty, my name is Toscano, I am the
commander of the Tressian army, and I carry
an urgent message from King Acri of Tressia.

Come forward and bring me this message.
Toscano, if all this is true, it must be stopped.
Your letter says you were at this camp, on
Elba. Will you lead my forces there?

Yes, your majesty.

We will leave at once.

The king's entourage and two wagons of
slaves and provisions were ready within

hours. We were given fresh horses, and soon the entire contingent was on our way to the port town of Piombino, a three-hour journey away.

The port was well protected in a narrow harbor, surrounded by thick walls, and it was well situated for defense against raiding from Greek pirates. A large Penteconter was docked along a stone pier jutting into the harbor. We were quickly all on board and set off for the island of Elba, directly across the strait.

We beached at Cavo, the same small fishing village I left a week earlier. The king had two scouts join Matteo, Nico, and me as we went ahead of the group to find the iron mining camp.

It was challenging and disorientating traveling through the tangled undergrowth. But after a few hours, we were at the camp. It was completely abandoned. The buildings emptied. Anything that could be carried away was gone. I went into the storage shed where I was detained and found all the amphoras were gone. All that remained was the hole in the ground where I was staked. When the king arrived, he doubted that iron was being mined here. I was desperate to find some evidence. I crawled headfirst, deep into the bottom of one of the furnaces, to find some. I needed a blade to free it, but a small mound of molten iron was lying in the back of the fire pit.

Your majesty, here is the proof of what was happening here. They're smelting iron ore mined from those mountains and forged into nuggets to be smuggled off the island. It has been going on here undetected for years.

How many men did you see working here?

When I arrived, there were four in the camp and dozens more working up in the mine.

Tell me what you know about them. What did you hear them say when they were detaining you?

They acted highly guarded as soon as they discovered me. It was long before I recognized that I had stumbled upon a smuggling undertaking. I just wasn't sure what it was they were smuggling. At one point, while I made my escape, I did hear one of them call out the name of their leader. They called him Atticus.

Atticus?

Yes, Atticus, that's the name I heard. Do you know of him, your majesty?

Unfortunately, I do. Years ago, I put him in charge of all the mining here on Elba. These mountains are full of copper, tin, silver, and even pockets of flint if you know where to look. He became a rich man, too rich. I heard rumors of him trading a part of the silver mined here to Greek privateers. He must have gotten word of this, and he disappeared before I could seize him, taking a sizable heap of silver with him.

His stash must be running low because he has returned. But now, he discovered something even more valuable than loads of silver, the iron deposits on the island. Although, I don't believe he is dealing with the Greeks any longer, and he is now collaborating with King Altare.

With this iron, this island has become even more valuable now.

I agree. King Altare would like nothing more than to take this island away from you and secure his source of this precious metal.

Your majesty, he may not stop just with this island. He could very well be after your entire kingdom. Knowing King Altare, he will not stop until he gets his way. That is why I am here. Together our two kingdoms can stop him.

You speak the truth, Toscano. He must be stopped. I will meet with your king.

CHAPTER 22: FATHER AND SON

Court of King Acri

Your majesty, the iron mining camp on Elba was abandoned when our expedition reached the island, but we did find evidence of iron being produced there. Here, look at this nugget, your majesty. It was dislodged from the bottom of a fire pit of one of the furnaces.

So, this is the metal that could change the world.

It has already begun, your majesty. In the hands of the right craftsman, it can be turned into a powerful fighting weapon, forged into a dense metal blade holding an extremely sharp edge. King Altare may have already obtained enough iron to supply his army with these new weapons. An alliance with

King Masterna may be the best way to prevent Altare from acquiring more and secure a supply for us. King Masterna knows that his kingdom is in no position to stop King Altare alone, so I believe he will be willing to join us for his protection.

Your majesty, securing this source of iron is but the first step. We must also understand and master the smelting process and the forging into weapons. There are only a few in Etruria who have this skill.

The men at the camp?

Yes, your majesty. The leader, Atticus, is one. But he will be the most difficult to get to aid us. There were others. I saw at least three other workers. I remember hearing one of their names. It was just after their guard dog attacked me. This Atticus was holding a sword at my back when he ordered one of his men to go back inside and get some cord. He said his name, but I am struggling to recall it. Sapu, yes, Sapu, that is it. He will be in Tarchina with the others. It should not be that difficult to find him. Atticus paid him well for the work they were doing. Finding a smithy with coins to spend in Tarchina will be easy. Persuading him to show us his skill shouldn't take more than offering him double the money that Atticus was paying him.

You must find him and bring him to me. Securing the ore from Elba would be worthless without the ability to smelt into iron.

Yes, your majesty. I will leave at dawn.

The City of Vetulonia, Court of King Mastarna

Your majesty, a messenger from Tarchina, seeks an audience with you.

Bring him to me.

Your majesty, I have an urgent message from King Altare. My name is Cintello, and my King bids you well and has sent me to discuss an arrangement with you.

On your knees and bow before me. Rise, Cintello, you serve your king well. Now, why has he not come himself with this urgent news?

He has complete faith in me, your majesty, and my words are his.

Go ahead. I am listening.

Your majesty, what you have learned is accurate; we trade for metal smuggled from Elba. But this was not our doing. We were approached by a trader called Atticus, a man from your city of Vetulonia. He offered us an astonishing new metal from the newly discovered ore mined in Etruria, found only on the island of Elba, one that could be forged into formidable weapons. We cannot afford to ignore this new metal, your majesty.

He and his men left your kingdom carrying the knowledge of turning this ore into iron weapons and are now in Tarchina. My King proposes an alliance between our two kingdoms that will bring us both enormous power and wealth. An equal partnership, offering each other what the other does not have.

What can you offer me? I will soon have control over these mines of this iron on Elba and do not need your help.

Yes, your kingdom presently holds a resource found nowhere else in Etruria, yet our kingdom knows how to turn this resource into fierce weapons. One is useless without the other. But for a fleeting time, together, we will be invincible.

What do you mean by this fleeting time? I alone have only access to this newly discovered metal. It's found only in one mine in all of Etruria.

That is true, your majesty, but for how long? How long do you think yours will be the only mine for this metal? Etruria is rich in resources, and our mountains hold countless amounts of valuable minerals. How long do you think it will be before more of this ore is found? Silver, tin, copper, and gold are never found in just one location. These metals are found in hundreds of mines in every part of our world, from Iberia to India. They all hold these precious metals, some in more abundance than others, but there is no one in sole possession of it all.

For now, our kingdom holds the knowledge of turning the ore into iron but keeping that a secret won't last long. We may be among the first here in Etruria, but the use of iron has been slowly spreading to all parts of the world. It has been in the hands of many great empires for hundreds of years. How long before every warrior in our league carries an iron sword? Our time is short, your majesty. The coming age of iron is upon us. We must use our advantage while we still have it.

What is it that your King proposing, exactly?

Allow us to re-open Camp Nell'elba. We'll train your blacksmiths in making iron at your furnaces there, and we will both have more iron than we will ever need.

I see. What I possess is far more valuable than what you hold, Cintello. Here is my only offer to you. Tarchina will have access to my mine for one year, and we will split evenly all the iron produced there. After one year, I alone take over all operations on Elba, and Tarchina will trade for its iron the same as everyone else.

A year? Do we have only a year? And you know about making iron forever?

As you said, Cintello, our time is fleeting, and it wouldn't be long before our advantage is lost. When will I have your answer from your King?

You will have your answer soon, your majesty.

Chambers of King Altare

Atticus, if we double your crew, is there enough iron ore in that mine on Elba to double your iron production for at least a year?

Your majesty, I would also need to add more furnaces, but the veins on Elba run deep, so even doubling the number of miners, they will not likely be exhausted for years.

Cintello, let King Masterna know we have a deal.

A Tavern in Tarchina

How will we find this Sapu?

Where would you go after working months, sweating in front of a blazing furnace, on a secluded island, with some coin in your pocket to burn?

To a place with tasty food and plenty to drink, served by curvy barmaids, and I wouldn't leave.

That's precisely the type of place where we are headed, Nico. But you're no longer Nico. You're a hardworking miner going by the name of Tarfu.

Tarfu?

Sure. You can call me Drusus. Let's go; Tarfu, our friend, is waiting.

How are you going to spot him?

A miner with money to burn will be easy to spot. We must get to him before his money runs out.

A Taven In Tarchina

Bartender, a mug of mead for me and my friend here; we're celebrating.

Celebrate what?

A hard day's work.

Congratulations, here's your mead.

That man over there, with that barmaid, looks familiar. Is his name Sapu? We worked the mines together on Elba.

Yes, that's him. He must have plenty to celebrate about also. He's been here for days.

Tarfu, let's get reacquainted with our friend.

Sapu? What are you doing here?

213

Who wants to know?

Sapu, are you drunk? How could you forget us? We busted our backs together. Remember?

And where was that?

Where? You are drunk. Let's go, Tarfu. Some forget their friends too quickly when they have cause to celebrate.

No, sit and join me. I am celebrating.

What's the occasion? Although you were never one that needed much of an excuse to drink.

I just got word that I'm going back to Elba. You wouldn't believe the find there, and it's easy digging.

Working for Atticus is never easy.

That's true. Do you know him?

Of course, we know him. What miner doesn't?

You two do look familiar. What did you say your name is?

You really don't remember us. I'm Drucius, and this is my brother, Tarfu. We're from Vetulonia. We've drank with you before, right here, not long ago. You don't remember us at all?

Refresh my memory and buy the next round.

Tarfu, toss over some coins while we get reacquainted with our friend here. When do you leave for Elba, Sapu?

What day is today? I leave on the first of the week.

Is there much work there?

Plenty, if you're willing to work hard. Are you looking for work? I could ask Atticus. He is always looking for good help. He pays well, and the food is decent.

That's kind of you, my friend. Let's drink to that! Another round here, on me!

Here's to Sapu!

No, here's to Atticus!

Sapu? You look a little uneasy, my friend. Are you getting sick?

What do you mean? I'm fine.

You don't look well. Let's get some air. It will do you good. Come on, easy now. Tarfu, give me a hand.

Where are we going?

Just outside.

What are you doing? Whose wagon is this? Where are we going?

Relax, Sapu, don't worry. Come with us; you are about to become a very wealthy man.

Court of King Acri

Your majesty, our guest, was very moved by your generous offer and has told us all we need to know. He has told us much about Campo Nell'elba's operation and how it is expanding and confirmed that King Mastarna made a deal with King Altare. It's a smart move, your majesty.

Yes, but one that has put us at a significant disadvantage. Commander, how fast do you think he will be able to learn to produce the iron we need?

Soon, your majesty. Sapu appreciates the gold he is being paid and is willing to share what he knows.

Good, keep me informed of the progress.

Lucien's Blacksmith Shop

Toscano, this is not working.

What do you mean, father?

All of it with Sapu. It is impossible to learn the process of making iron from him. It's not something someone can tell you. You must do it yourself, many times, with guidance all along the way, for the smelting to be successful. It's a skill that takes time to master. You must learn many things: bellowing the fire to get the temperature hot enough, adding the correct quantity of charcoal, bathing to cool and harden, re-heating, tamping, and folding the ore into a blade. It all must be done precisely. You have seen me working metal. Each is quite different.

Toscano, you know that smithing is an art and a science, taking years of apprenticeship before you can master it. With new metal, you must learn every step of the process from beginning to end. This Sapu is a poor teacher. He's just an assistant and not genuinely knowledgeable. Plus, I have no iron ore here. How am I going to learn without it? I need to know by doing.

I see your point, father. Let's go to speak to the King.

Chambers of King Acri

I understand, and it is more of a process than I realized. Then, Lucine, you will do it yourself.

How can I, your majesty? I do not have the oar and have not mastered the technique. There is no ore here.

Then you will go where it is and learn how it is done there.

To Elba?

Yes, and Toscano will go with you. You will go there and learn all you need to know for yourself. You wouldn't stay long. Just long enough for you to master the skill yourself.

Your majesty, there will be much suspicion surrounding my father on Elba once they learn he is from Tressia. His life could be in danger.

Yes, you and he must both be careful. This is the only way. Without this knowledge, soon, all our lives will be in danger. I have arranged to have Fasti at his side, and you will remain close to them on the island.

Your majesty, he has never done anything like this before.

Toscano, it will be fine. I will go, your majesty.

Good, it is settled. Toscano, Fasti will make a fine bodyguard for your father. He has worked in the mines before. With your father's skills, I am sure it will not be difficult for them to fit in at the camp.

You leave for Piombino on the morning tide. As you know, it's a short journey across the straits to Camp Nell'elba from there. Toscano, you are to stay behind at Piombino and make your way to the island later. You may be recognized, so you must remain hidden and rendezvous with them outside the Camp.

Once your father has learned what he needs to know, bring them back to Piombino. The ship will remain there waiting for all of you.

Lucien, how long will you need at the mining camp?

A week, two at most, your majesty.

Good.

Your majesty, once we return, we still need a source of the ore to produce the iron.

And I will make sure you have it. The metal-bearing hills of Colline Metallifere are sure to hold iron ore veins, as do the mountains on Elba. They are in the same mountain range, and we now know what the veins look like. May the gods bestow good fortune on your mission.

On The Ship To Piombino

Father, do you remember the last time we were on a journey together?

Of course, you were just a boy. I took you to your first spring festival at Fanum Voltumnae.

That was the first time I saw the sea.

I remember.

Those memories are still strong in me and have helped me through some tough times.

They are strong with me also; I remember that time as well. That is when I realized you had turned from a boy into a man. You were brave enough to choose the destiny you wanted, not the one I planned for you.

And you didn't stop me, father. I thank you to this day.

I will be glad I didn't when we both get back to Tressia in one piece.

We will, father. We both are good at what we do.

See, there is no stopping you, Toscano.

There's no stopping us, father. Father, when you and your guard Fasti reach the camp, you must talk to Atticus. Persuade him that you have the blacksmithing skills he can use with your talents that will not be difficult. There is a place at the far end of the camp behind the furthest furnace where we can meet. I will be there waiting every midnight. Father, I'll be watching you the entire time. At the first sign of trouble, Fasti knows what to do.

It will be fine, do not be concerned. I know how to manage myself, Toscano. We'll meet when the time is right.

Piombino Harbor

We are looking to cross to the island, can you take us?

What is your business on Elba?

We're miners looking for work. I hear there is work to be found at Camp Nell'elba. Can you take us there?

The mining camp is on the other side of the island. It will be ten coins each to take you both there.

Ten coins each?

Yes, unless you'd both like to swim. Ask for Atticus. The last I heard, he was still looking for men.

Campo Nell'elba

Where can I find Atticus?

Who is asking?

The best smithy in all of Etruria.

Oh, really?

Now bring us to him, or I will take my skills elsewhere.

What's your name, smithy?

Lucien, formally of Tressia.

Tressia?

Yes, I have moved on from there.

Why so?

The ladies were insisting I was their baby's father.

How many ladies?

Too many, now bring me to Atticus.

Atticus, this man, claims to be the best smithy in all of Etruria.

Then that would make you better than me.

It would.

What is your name, blacksmith, and who is this with you?

My name is Lucien, and this man is with me. He is my assistant, Fasti.

Come with me, smithy Lucien, show me what you can do with this copper ore here.

It looks like there is enough ore here for one dagger. Come back in two hours.

This is nicely done, Lucien.

Tell me about the metal being smelted over there. Iron, isn't it?

How did you hear of it?

That is why I am here. Word spreads fast. It would be hard to find a blacksmith in all of Etruria that has not heard about it. I've wanted to work with this metal since I held a sword made of Damascus steel. It was magnificent, beautiful to the eye, and deadly in the hands of the proper warrior. I could make a sword of steel if I could only get some of that ore and learn the secrets of smelting it.

Well, we are mining and smelting iron ore by the basket full. But refining the iron into a useful steel weapon has eluded us.

Show me how you smelt it, and we may be able to help each other.

Come, follow me, and I'll show you.

This metal is strong and much more robust than copper or bronze. But it's far too brittle.

Atticus, let's try adding to the number of cooling baths. But let's try reheating this next batch even hotter, 'till it glows white, then we'll quickly plunge it back into the water.

Yes, that is much better, Lucien.

When did you first learn about iron and smelting ore?

It is a long story and goes back to my childhood on Crete.

That's fine. I'm not going anywhere.

Well, my father was Greek from the colony of Cumae. He was an olive oil trader, among other things. When I was old enough, we sailed together all over the Aegean. On one of those trips, we landed in Crete. There, I saw an iron sword being forged for the first time. I was fascinated. I begged my father to arrange an apprenticeship for me the following year. I lived in Crete for three years, learning all I could before sailing for home. It was on my journey back home when

Etruscan pirates attacked us. My father was killed in the fighting, and I was captured and sold as a slave in Tarchina. I worked in the copper mines in the hills surrounding the city at Sorgere Minerale for years. I would occasionally make deliveries of the copper ore to the blacksmith of the King. I soon befriended him. He was amazed when I told him about the iron ore in Crete. It was not long before the King learned of this, and I found myself working for him and eventually landing here.

Campo Nell 'Elba

I sat patiently waiting at our rendezvous spot just outside the camp. It was now well past midnight, and my father and Fasti had still not arrived. If I waited any longer, we would never make it to Piombino before dawn. I had no choice but to move into the camp to find them. As I stepped closer, I could hear voices coming from one of the dwellings. Crouching below the window, the noises I heard turned out to be awful singing, and judging by his voice, it was coming from Atticus. Peering into the dimly lit room, I could see my father sitting at a table in the center next to Fasti. They had been drinking for a while. I could smell the sweet wine from where I was crouched beneath the window outside.

I needed to get my father's attention, he was only a few feet away, but he was facing away with his back toward me. Frustrated, I began to toss pebbles at his back through the window, but he didn't budge. Finally, I threw one that hit him hard on the back of his head. He quickly turned around and noticed me. I was frantically motioning to him to go to the door. He got up from his chair, saying he had to relieve himself, and I met him behind the building.

It's time to end this farewell party, father.

I know. I tried to leave a few times, but Atticus insisted we keep drinking to celebrate our remarkable work. I have never seen anyone drink that much wine.

Father, we need to end this party now. Go back in there and get Fasti and say you must leave. You're not feeling well.

They made their exit, leaving Atticus half asleep on the bed. We headed out of the camp towards the fishing boat I had waiting for us on the beach.

Father, where are you going? Father?

Stay here. I must go back.

Why?

Just stay here. I'll be right back.

Father, no, we must go.

It wouldn't take long.

What's that?

Look at this. It's my first iron sword. No way was I leaving it behind.

Can we go? We should be able to make it back to Piombino by dawn if we are lucky.

The boat was there right where we had left it. My father, Fasti, and I jumped in and shoved off. The tide had turned, and the rowing was slow and laborious. The seas were getting rough as the wind picked up and turned against us when we reached the bay's open waters. We took turns at the oars trying to fight the seas and reach the mainland as soon as possible. It was dawn, and we were still at least three miles from the coastline. It would be another hour of hard rowing before we finally reached Piombino harbor. We awoke the sleeping crew of our waiting ship and were soon on our way back to Tressia.

Campo Nell' Elba

Where's Lucien and that Fasti?

They're gone, Atticus, and they took that sword he made with them. Should we go after them?

They're halfway to Piombino by now. Not a word of this to anyone, Supa. Let's get to work. We have a new sword to make for the king.

Villa Feonia

Gia, they have discovered iron in a mine at Colline Metallifere.

What does this mean, Toscano?

It means that my father will soon have the iron he needs to produce the weapons for our defense.

Are you expecting us to be at war soon?

It is inevitable. King Altare, with his new ally, Vulci, will want revenge for his defeat at Poggio Fichina. War is sure to come this spring.

Court of King Acri

May I present you with my first sword crafted in iron?

It's a fine weapon Lucien, thank you. How long did you work to produce it?

227

With the ore and furnace at my disposal, it was a full day's work, your majesty.

It is an excellent weapon.

It is my first, your majesty, so I had much to learn about the smelting and forging of the iron, refining my technique many times before it was completed.

Let's assume it is needed quicker. With assistance, how many swords of this quality could you make in a day?

If I had much aid, your majesty, workers to supply and stoke the charcoal for the high heat needed, metalsmiths to help smelt the ore, blacksmiths to fold and tamp the iron, then bathe, grind and sharpen the blades. With all working together, we could produce ten to fifteen swords a day from one furnace.

So, you could produce forty to fifty of these swords daily with four furnaces and enough skilled workers?

Your majesty, this is all new. Many will need time to acquire the necessary skills, as I did. But I could produce close to those numbers daily once the training was completed, and I had four furnaces and all the materials and artisans needed.

Lucien, how many artisans do you estimate will be needed per furnace? I will not hold you to the exact number. Your best judgment, Lucien?

My lord, we have four furnaces operating. Each would need eight to ten workers to produce that quantity.

Lucien, you will have four furnaces, fifty craftsmen, and all the wood and iron ore you'll need. My master-builder, Pesna, is ready to begin building your furnaces at a new mining camp at Colline Metallifere. You can describe to him what he needs to do, and it will be done. Lucien, you have the full powers of this king behind you. I was hoping you could do your best to get me my swords within the month.

Camp Colline Metallifere

Pesna, the stones must form a circle, three paces in diameter, and the burning chamber must start here and be raised here.

Father, you have progressed well since I was here last. It looks like the king will have his swords in plenty of time.

He will. And we'll be producing other iron weapons as well. We should be ready to show him within the week.

Which will be first?

Which weapon do you prefer, Commander?

First should be the gladii, followed by the javelins and then the shields.

Chambers of King Acri

These weapons are magnificent, Lucien. We must have these weapons in the hands of our first line of infantry as soon as possible.

How many would you need, your majesty?

For our first line, the number would be fifty.

Fifty? By when?

Within the month, war will soon be upon us, Lucien.

I will need more workers, your majesty, at least twenty here in the camp and ten more in the mines.

You will have them.

Camp Colline Metallifere

Father, come, enough for today, come. The light will be gone anyway, and Gia expects us back at the villa. And your grandson, he has not seen you in a week.

I must stay a while longer. There is too much to be done.

Father, come. It will be here waiting for you in the morning.

Fine, the thought of seeing my grandson is reason enough. He reminded me of you when you were his age. But he may be even brighter.

He is. Now, father, let's go.

Villa Fionia

Gia, we need to talk.

About what?

I want you and Donato to stay with my parents in Tressia for a while.

Leave the villa? Why?

It's becoming too dangerous.

What do you mean? We have the company of scouts right here. You said we would be safe here.

Normally you would, but not now. War is coming, and a company of scouts will not be enough to protect you here.

When? When do we leave?

In two days. All the servants, too. Give them no cause for alarm. Tell them it is time for Donato to visit the city.

Does your father know?

Yes, I have already spoken to him.

Sanctuary of Tarchina

What do you see? What are the gods saying about the future? About war with Tarchina?

My lord, listen, the god Laran is speaking to me. He speaks of a colossal battle, many will die, and we must be prepared to sacrifice in his honor.

When? When will this battle be? Who will be victorious?

He does not reveal that to me. Only that you must not fight until his festival has passed. Now you must go, and he speaks to me no more.

Chambers of King Altare

My lord, our spies in Tressia, have confirmed that iron is mined at Colline Metallifere, and a large camp produces many weapons there.

How is it possible that they have learned about iron so quickly?

There must be a traitor, my lord, at Campo Nell'elba. That's the only way.

Cintello, go there and find out how this could have happened.

Yes, my lord.

Campo Nell'elba

Atticus, I see you have added three more furnaces to the camp. Any problems in increasing the output of the iron?

No problem, I can't manage, Cintello. It all goes well. As the King requested, we're doubling the iron we produce.

Good, so where did you find the men necessary to work the new furnaces?

It wasn't difficult. The word was spread in town.

Who are these men? I want to meet them.

Of course, follow me. We have added close to twenty now.

I see. And all the men you have recently hired here? Have any not worked out?

There are always a few laggards that must be weeded out.

How many was that?

There were two.

What were their names, and where were they from?

They were miners from Tressia by the names of Lucien and Fasti.

Did you hire men from Tressia?

They said they were forced to leave.

And you believed them?

They were good workers.

Then why aren't they here?

They left.

You let them go? After they worked here and learned what we were doing?

They slipped out of camp in the middle of the night.

You fool! They were spies, and you trusted them.

How can you be so sure?

Were they eager to learn from you how to treat the ore to make the iron?

One of them was.

Was he a skilled blacksmith?

He was.

Then, I am sure. As we suspected, you have exposed this entire operation, Atticus; the King will not be pleased.

Chambers of King Acri

My lord, scouts have spotted the army of King Altare. It has left Tarchina and is heading north.

Where did he spot them?

A three-day march from here, my lord.

How many?

He reported over a thousand men, my lord.

Is your plan ready?

It is my lord.

Let's hear it.

With that force that large, he could lay siege on the city for months and starve us to death. We must meet him on the field, my lord.

Please go on. I'm listening.

It's best to meet him at a place we chose, where we will hold the high ground in a solid, defensible position. My lord, the soil is still wet and muddy in many places this early in spring. Our marshes to the north are saturated and unpassable, making it impossible to attack us from that direction.

Here you can see the three viable routes approaching us from the south, the Fosso Rigo, Torrente Rio, and the Fosso Acqua. Each of them has positions where we could be waiting, which will give us a strategic advantage. The middle path following the Torrente Rio is the least likely. It is still soft from the rain and snow melt, making it thick with mud and impassable in the lower spots. He will likely travel from the west following Fosso Rigo or east along the Fosso Acqua.

If we arrive first and hold the high ground here or here, with this advantage, he will want us to attack him. So, we must remain patient and resist, wait him out, your majesty. He is on our soil with limited supplies. The longer he waits, the more foraging he will need to do to feed his army. We will send out raiding parties to ambush and harass them, making it dangerous and difficult for them. He will eventually be forced to attack first or leave. Knowing King Altare, he will attack.

Our formation will be tight, with two companies deep and four across and an additional two companies of cavalry and one infantry held in reserve. Our flanks will be protected, stretching from tree line to tree line. His attack will begin with his archers and javelins. But we will be ready with our shields locked in the testudo, giving us cover with most of his arrows and javelins being deflected. When their volley is finished, we return fire. He will then attack our lines with his cavalry, looking for weakness before advancing his infantry.

But we will remain strong, with our new iron weapons versing his. He will order multiple advances, but we will hold, replacing our fallen men with those stationed behind them. His men will be forced to repeatedly climb up to the high ground, struggling with footing and growing tired with each advance.

We hold fast until their third advance. Then our center will start cave, slowly falling back, giving ground, creating the appearance of a weakness in the middle of our formation. It will be too tempting an opportunity for King Altare to resist. He will concentrate his infantry and rush towards the center, attempting to push through our line and break us. But our men will not be retreating in panic. They will slide into either side of our line, forming a fortified corridor.

As his infantry is drawn into the gap, we will charge at them with our cavalry. With the favor of the gods, we will rout them right there.

This plan is a good one, Commander. Have your men been made ready to implement these tactics?

Yes, your majesty, we have been preparing for this maneuver for the last three weeks. They're ready.

Commander, be ready to move out tomorrow.

Fosso Rigo Trail

Commander, the Tarchinian army is headed right toward us.

How far are they, Matteo?

Ten miles, Commander. More than enough time for us to reach the hilltop as planned.

Have our scouts continue to track them and report back every hour.

Yes, Commander.

Fosso Rigo Hilltop

Matteo, have the troops fall into formation, with the forward line stationed right here, on the crest of the hill.

Yes, Commander.

What is the latest position on the Tarchinian forces?

They're five miles back, heading up the Fosso Rigo route toward us. If they continue at their current pace, they'll reach us within the hour.

They're here, Commander.

They'll stop and set their lines just beyond the range of our archers.

Commander, as you predicted, they're spreading out in formation just beyond range.

Our scout seems to have overestimated their numbers. They don't look close to the thousand in strength he first reported. How many do you estimate, Matteo?

I agree, Commander. They look to be well under a thousand.

Bring that scout to me.

Is this the size of the army you spotted marching out of Tarchina?

No Commander. It doesn't look like the size of the entire army I saw leaving Tarchina.

Matteo, have our scouts comb the surrounding woodlands. They must have split their army along their route and are trying to outflank us.

Commander, the sun will be setting soon, and they still are not advancing.

We hold the high ground as planned, Matteo. What do you hear from our scouts?

All but one, Commander, have reported, and they have not seen any signs of flanking enemy troops.

Where did this one scout go missing?

On our right flank, Commander.

Send two scouts to our right flank and have our cavalry unit ready to advance if they are stopped.

Yes, Commander.

Commander, their archers, they have begun to move forward.

Soldiers of Tressia, you see men coming towards us who have invaded our land. They are here with the intent to butcher and enslave us. They are here to destroy our homes and brutalize our families. We stand together here, on this very spot, to stop them! Hold tight to our plan, and we will crush them. We will show them what it means to be Tressian. Together, we fight for our homes! Together, we fight for our families! Together we fight for our king! Together, we will destroy them! Trissians, together we will send them straight to hell!

Men, hold steady now. Hold right where you are. Ready shields! Raise shields! Archers ready, Archers, fire!

The sky was soon darkened by hundreds of arrows flying in waves in both directions. Our men in the first line knelt with their shields over them as a barrage of arrows came raining down on them. Most were glancing off their iron-clad shields, but some managed to hit their mark. I could see our arrows inflicted even more severe damage on their lightly armored archers, and they soon fell back.

Their cavalry was next to charge. They galloped up the hill, but their speed was slowed by muddy ground and the steepness of the incline. I could hear Matteo give the order for the front line to kneel and anchor their shields into the ground, creating an almost impregnable wall. The Trachinian cavalry soon pummeled straight into it. Some burst through, knocking down our men and trampling over them as they moved forward. But many lost their momentum as they hit up against the wall and slowed enough to be attacked from the sides, pulled off their mounts, and slaughtered on the ground. Their remaining cavalry withdrew. It was now set for the infantry to try an attack. With screams of terror, they charged up the slope.

Our front remained intact and continued to defy their advances, filling in the gaps of the fallen men with fresh troops from deeper within the formation.

The fighting was fierce, men falling on both sides, but our lines held, and the Tarchinian infantry was continually forced to retreat. The infantry attack was now intermingled with the Tarchinian cavalry for their next charge. Matteo quickly ordered our long lances to be anchored to the ground behind the front line. As their horses charged our position, many lances pierced straight into them. Riders were thrown off their mounts, many crushed by their horse falling on top of them.

It wasn't long before they reformed to mount a third charge. The attack was fierce, and Matteo ordered the battle horn to sound the first maneuver. The infantry in the center gradually began to give way. Sensing an area of weakness, the Tarchinains concentrated their attack on our center, and the stage was set.

The battle horn now sounded for our infantry to form shield walls on each side of the corridor, setting the trap. It was time for our cavalry units to charge the center, and we rushed straight into the advancing Tarchinian infantry. They were shocked when they realized they were now surrounded on three sides, and with little chance of repelling a cavalry assault, they turned and began to run.

Right then, I heard clashes of iron and cries of battle coming from behind me. As I turned, I saw our reserve units being attacked by the missing portion of the Tarchinian army. They were outnumbered five to one. In the center of the fighting, I could see Nico rally his men, surrounding the king, to make a stand.

I rushed towards them, leading a small cavalry group that held a position near me. I plowed through the fighting to get to Nico. I dove off my horse when I reached him, taking two men down with me. I grabbed a sword and pounced on anyone who moved toward me. The fighting was savage, chaotic, hand-to-hand combat. As it raged, more of our men pushed in to join the fight. Eventually, we started to gain control of the area, and the surviving Tarchinians still standing began to break and flee. Men were lying everywhere. I frantically screamed for Nico, searching for him among the dead and wounded, but there was no answer. Nor was I able to locate the king. Then off to my right, I saw an arm raised and heard Nico's voice calling out to me.

Nico, I'm here. Can you hear me, Nico?

Toscano, I can't move my legs. I'm scared.

It's fine, Nico. I'm here with you, my brother. Hold my hand. I'm not leaving you. Nico, hold on tight.

243

It can't feel anything, Toscano.

I know Nico, I'm staying with you right here.
Look at me. I'm right here, brother.

You'll always be my big brother, Toscano.
Vera, take care of her, Toscano.

I'm so proud of you, my brother. You are
indeed the brave one. Nico. Nico. Don't go.
Nico? Nico? I'm so sorry. I love you.

Toscano, he has gone. I'm so sorry,
Commander. He's gone. Come, Commander,
we must leave.

Matteo, I should have protected him. My
brother and king are dead because of me, and
I could have saved them. They are dead,
Matteo, and I did it. They're both dead
because of me.

Commander, you did not kill them. It's war,
Commander, and good men die. You did all
you could.

I should have done more.

You won the war, Commander. We defeated a
much larger and better-equipped army. You
saved Tressia. No one could have done what
you just did, Commander, no one. Nico, the
King, and all the men died here with honor,
saving their home.

I should have known they would divide their
army.

They did, and it cost them the victory, Commander. They didn't have the numbers to break our front lines. You know it's true, Commander.

Look at all these men, Matteo. Look at all that was sacrificed.

Our men gave their lives so others could live, Commander. They are heroes who will not be forgotten. We have won, Commander. It is all over now.

This is not over. If King Altare lives, this war is not over, and it will never be over until I kill him. Where is he, Matteo?

He fled the field when he saw our cavalry was routing his infantry.

We must hunt him down. He does not get to live while my brother, king, and all these men are dead. How many were with him when he fled?

Twenty at the most, Commander.

Assemble a dozen of our fastest cavalry archers, and we leave at once.

Fosso Rigo Trail

He'll be riding hard to make it back to the safety of Tarchina. It's at least a three-day journey from here. He'll have to stop for water, feed, and rest his horses. The safest

245

place for him to do this is in Vulci. If we take the Fasso Rigo path, we could ambush him there before he reaches the city.

The Fasso Rigo? Are you sure, Commander? That's more of a goat trail than a road. It can be very treacherous in places. It will be challenging to move quickly.

But it is the shortest path to Vulci. If the gods are with us, we can cut him off before he gets by.

Commander, the heavy rains have badly eroded the trail ahead, and there's barely any footing.

Dismount. We lead the horses from here. Slowly, men follow me.

Stop! This is the perfect place to set the ambush. Matteo, take three men to the ravine's other side. Have them take positions among those outcropping there. When you hear my signal, we unleash an onslaught of arrows on the riders below. But Matteo, tell your men I want the king to be taken alive.

They're approaching, Commander.

Get ready, men. Aim, steady, Fire!

There is no place to run, your majesty. Get down off your mount. It will be just you and me. We have a score to settle.

Commander Toscano, we finally met. We can settle this like men. I can make you extremely wealthy, Commander. I have more gold than you've ever seen and more land than you need. Just give me the word, and it'll all be yours. You will be a wealthy man, Toscano. You will be a king.

No amount of your blood money can save you, your majesty. All your dirty money cannot pay for what you have done. Your debt to me will only be satisfied when I send you to hell, where you belong. Now here, pick up that sword, defend yourself. It's your only chance of remaining alive.

No! Please!

This is for all you have killed, your majesty. Now, your debt is settled.

Villa Feonia

Toscano, praise to the gods; you're alive. My dreams were full of death. I could not sleep. I felt death all around me. It has been horrible since you've been gone. Nico? Where's Nico? Is he with you? Toscano, where is he? Where's Nico?

He died a warrior, Gia, in my arms.

Oh, Toscano, I'm so sorry, so, so sorry. I know how much you loved him and how he loved you. You were a great brother to him, Toscano. He looked up to you. He was so proud of you. I'm so sorry.

And I was so proud of him. There's a pain deep in my heart, and it won't stop. I'll miss him forever. I must go. I must go and tell my parents.

Hold on. I will go with you.

Toscano, you are back! Where's Nico? What has happened? No, my gods, no! My son, my poor son.

He died a warrior in my arms, mother. I should've never let him die. I should never have allowed him to join me. He is dead now because of me, and I couldn't save him. It's my fault he's gone.

No, no, my son. Following you is what he wished to do. You nor I could tell him how to live his life. He was a man making his own choices and living as he wanted. There was no way he was not joining you.

You mustn't blame yourself, Toscano. No one is to blame, and it's no one's fault. The gods have willed this so.

I miss him, father.

I know my son. We all will miss him. You were a great brother to him.

And was he a great brother to me. I can't bear the thought that he is gone.

We will all bear his loss together.

Where's Vera? I must be the one to tell her.

Toscano, what is wrong? Where is Nico? Oh no! Toscano, my gods.

I am so sorry, Vera.

It can't be, it can't be, my Nico, oh my poor Nico. No!

I am so sorry, Vera. He died a hero in my arms, saving many lives, including mine. He rests with the gods in heaven, and they will honor him for his courage.

Oh, my gods, no!

Vera, come, come with me inside. You must rest.

My Nico, Oh my gods, my poor Nico. My Nico, he's gone. I loved him so much, Gia.

I know. I'm so sorry, Vera. He'll always be with us in our hearts, and the gods will reward him for his sacrifice.

They have already.

What do you mean?

I have their reward, Gia. I carry his child.

Praise the gods! Vera! I am so happy for you, Vera. Nico lives inside you.

Toscano, come quick, Vera; she carries Nico's child.

The gods have eased our pain. They honor him and us. It is so wonderful, Vera. You are blessed. We are all blessed. Praise the gods.

The Court of Tressia

Toscano, you have built and led our army. You have fought bravely and sacrificed your only brother, saving our kingdom. Toscano, you have done all that has been asked of you and more, faithfully serving Tressia and our king.

I have done what any true soldier would do.

You have done much more than that, Commander. King Acri trusted you, and we trust you also. Our king has left instructions for a successor if he were to die without an heir, and Toscano, the king, has named you as his successor.

I am no king, magistrate.

You need not be. It has been decided that King Acri will be the last of the kings of Tressia. The council has agreed that a king will no longer rule Tressia. The council of magistrates is to elect the next ruler, Zilath, the ruler of Tressia, for one year. Toscano, in the name of our great king and the people of

Tressia, the council of magistrates has elected you to be the first Zilath of Tressia.

Magistrates, I am not worthy of such an honor, and I am a warrior and not skilled in the demands of governing.

We humbly disagree, Toscano. We have seen you lead and inspire many. You have obtained safety and stability for Tressia. You have the faith of the people. The transition from a kingdom requires a man such as you. The king knew you would make a great ruler. We agree and implore you to accept the position of Zilath and lead us forward for one year. Toscano, Tressia, your city, needs you.

Magistrates, I am honored by your faith in me to govern the people of Tressia. To honor and respect the wishes of our past king, I will accept the position of Zilath of the council.

Praise to the gods. We have our Zilath.

As Zilath, one of my first duties was to represent Tressia at an unusual fall meeting of the League of Twelve Peoples. An urgent gathering at Fanum Voltumnae was called to decide on a crucial request being brought before the council by the city of Veii. Their king has asked the League to join them in their war with Rome.

Fanum Voltumnae

It was King Vel Saties of Vulci's turn to lead the council. He called upon Lars Tolumnus, King of Veii, to address the council. The king spoke of the war raging for more than ten years between Rome and Veii, along with its allied cities of Tarquinii and Caere. But the balance of power has now turned in Rome's favor. Since gaining control over many cities of the Latin League, Rome has been able to extract tribute from them, gaining men and arms in exchange for peace. Rome now has acquired the strength to lay an extended siege upon Veii. King Tolumnus has called upon the League for desperately needed assistance to break this siege and win victory over Rome.

My fellow Etruscans, I am here because the proud Etruscan city of Veii urgently needs your help. Veii, along with our neighbors Tarquinii and Caere, has been battling a ruthless, cruel enemy for decades. But now, this enemy has grown stronger, conquering and controlling all the tribes of their Latin League. It has strengthened where even the joint power of three of the wealthiest cities of the League is still not enough to defeat her. Unless our entire League unites to battle this enemy, we and soon all of us will be destroyed by Rome. It will take a strong, unified army from Etruria to stop her. If we do not join as one now and unite our troops to defeat Rome, the once-great Etruscan people will be no more.

King Porsenna of Vetulonia was next to speak.

King Tolumnus speaks of this war. Isn't he who has brought it upon himself? Wasn't it he who murdered four Roman ambassadors who were seeking peace? Wasn't it he who allied himself with the revolt against Rome in the nearby Roman colony of Fidenae? Wasn't he who instigated a war with Rome by seizing sizable portions of land along the Tiber that belonged to Rome for decades? Rome is home to many Etruscans; it is more of an Etruscan city than many realized. This war is a fight among neighbors and should be fought only by those involved. The blood of the entire League should not be spilled in a neighborhood fight.

The council was in an uproar, with voices extolling both sides of the issue. Many shouted that if Veii were left unaided, it would undoubtedly fall to Rome. Rome had to stop, and there was no end to its ambitions. With Veii destroyed, Caere Tarquinii, Vulci, Tarchina, or even Tressia would follow. Others agreed with King Porsenna of Vetulonia, believing it was a local matter among neighboring cities and should be settled by them. The other cities of the League are not threatened nor in danger and should not be involved.

It was now my turn to speak.

Over the last twenty years, at least a dozen wars have been raging between these two cities. Veii, for centuries, one of the wealthiest cities in our League, prospering from trading up and down the Tiber to the far reaches of the Mediterranean, now it finds itself fighting for its very existence. For years Rome was just one of the many remote and fledgling Latin cities, even being ruled for generations by Etruscan kings. But it has strengthened, colonized, or annexed any neighboring Latin cities. It now has the strength that rivals any of our cities, and its ambitions are growing. There is indeed blamed for being shared as to the cause of this current war. But Rome has shown that its unrelenting desire to rule us all is the true motivation for waging war. I know all of us here wish for peace, just and lasting peace for all of Etruria. But history has proven that Rome will only seek peace when it has had its way and all of us have been conquered.

Fellow Etruscans, together today, we still have the power to stop Rome. If we remain unmoved by King Tolumnus and stand by while his city falls, we will witness only the first of our cities to be conquered by Rome. The fate of all Etruria is resting in your hands. We must unite and put down this rising aggressor, or we will all end up dominated by her.

Although many rose to their feet in applause, the council could not reach a decision. It called on the high priest to petition the deities for a solution, and the proceedings were moved to the temple of Voltumnae. At

the temple altar, the High Priest Jovan
demanded the gods for the appropriate
response. According to the signs revealed in
the animals he sacrificed, the High Priest
decreed that the gods favored the decision to
abandon Veii and leave it to its destiny.

King Tolumnus stormed out of the temple,
knowing he had little chance of surviving.
Veii withstood the Roman siege for another
two years, but eventually, Rome sacked the
city. The Roman General Camillus devised a
plan to drain the trenches surrounding the
city walls and dig beneath them to storm into
the city.

When news of the fall of Veii reached Tressia,
the city, like the rest of Etruria, was in shock.
If a powerful city such as Veii could fall to
Rome, all of Etruria was threatened.

When my one-year term as Zilath ended, I remained a consul member and resumed my duties as commander of the Tressian army. The city was still at peace but remained in a difficult position with the menacing Romans not far to the south and a growing Gallic Senones tribe settling in the Po valley to our northeast, fast becoming a problem. If the League of Twelve allowed Veii to fall to the Romans, it could not be counted on to defend any Etruscan city. Tressia was on its own and needed to forge alliances if it were to endure.

Chambers of the Zilath of Tressia

Zilath Rasnal, may I speak freely?

Certainly, Commander.

As you know, we face potent enemies both north and south, and we do not have the strength to defeat either of them alone. Our best action is to form alliances with one of them and be ready when war does come.

Which of these do you suggest?

257

Rome, my Zilath. They continue to strengthen and pose a growing threat. We can secure our peace and enlist their support if we ally with them.

I can see the wisdom in your proposal. But what would Rome need of us?

They, too, have many enemies and can be defeated if they unite against them. Securing us as an ally would allow them at least one secure border and enable them to concentrate on more potent enemies.

I will bring it before the council.

Zilath, I have one more favor to ask.

Go ahead, Commander.

I ask that you do not make your position known until all have spoken first. I want each consul member the opportunity to commit independently. That will give us the firmest resolve.

You have my word, Commander.

Thank you, Zilath.

Tressian Barracks

Matteo, we are taking a trip to Rome.

Where?

To Rome, we are to be emissaries of Tressia for a mission there.

May I ask, Commander, for what purpose is this mission?

It is to secure an alliance with Rome.

Commander, who would suggest such a thing?

I did.

Commander, are you sure this is wise?

Matteo, Tressia has grown into a wealthy, prospering city in a land full of rich mineral resources, backed by a formidable army we have developed. But we are one city, and as we have seen, our foes can gather in much greater numbers, and we cannot rely upon our League for any protection. We must look elsewhere. Forging foreign alliances is a way to secure our safety. Rome has grown into a powerful military force. We will have one less foe to contend with if we are allies.

Commander, how long can we trust Rome? How long before they betray us as they have done to many already?

We will make it long, Matteo. We are going to propose a thirty-year truce between our two cities. If we use this time wisely and forge an actual Etruscan League uniting all our cities under one mighty army, Tressia and our culture will have a chance to survive Rome.

Villa Feonia

Toscano, how can you be sure the Roman Senate will not have you killed when you arrive?

Gia, there is no way to be sure, but our messenger was well-received, returning with an invitation for us to speak before the Senate. If they were to kill anyone, it would have been him. I believe they will be interested in what we offer. Rome has fought for decades to gain wealth and power, but they have also been strengthened by cultivating numerous alliances.

The City of Rome

After a five-day journey to Rome, the thickly forested mountain path finally opened on the last evening. I could now see an endless series of rolling hills, shallow valleys, and meandering streams stretching to the horizon. As we descended further, we became immersed in thick groves of olive trees, followed closely by acres of vineyards. The vines were draped with juicy ruby red, ripening grapes. I couldn't resist and moved off the trail to get close and reached down to grab a handful as I went by. Continuing down the sloop, we passed through vast expanses of grazing pastures and tracts of farmland filled with hectares of wheat and barley. As the road continued, we meandered through small villages with farmhouses surrounded by pens filled with cattle, goats, hogs, and sheep. Enough crops and animals were being grown here to feed ten cities the size of Tressia.

As we traveled closer to Rome, the surrounding countryside was dotted with larger towns containing workshops, taverns, and stables. Looking out in front of us, I could now see the outline of the city. Soon temples and large villas appeared on the hillsides, glistening in the hot afternoon sun. Rome was already looking much more extensive than I had imagined. As we approached the city gates, I was surprised to see it bound by earthen embankments, topped only with a wooden stockade barricading the city. But once inside, it was much grander than any Etruscan city. The streets were winding, paved with stone, and lined with stone and brick homes and shops, two and three stories high in places. A high-arched aqueduct led into the city, feeding the many ornate fountains scattered around the city squares. People congregated, drinking and filling containers at many of these fountains. As we traveled further, we passed an impressive marble building containing public baths. It had lines of citizens assembled in front, waiting to enter. As we moved further into the city, the streets were teeming with people, and the air was saturated with all types of smells and sounds, combining to create a hectic and bustling metropolis.

We stopped in front of a stable, where Matteo and I dismounted. Since Matteo was much more fluent in Latin than I was, he was the first to ask the proprietor for directions to the Forum. As we walked the streets, every inch of space was filled with stone buildings, two or three stories high. Up ahead, in a valley between two hills, I could see the gates of the Circus Maximus. It was the most impressive wood and brick structure I have ever seen, much more commanding than the circus at Fanum Voltumnae. It looked spacious enough to hold more than ten thousand spectators. Moving a few blocks further, the Forum came into view. At one end stood the majestic Senate building, rising nobly on a small plateau. It was bounded in front by a row of gleaming white, polished marble columns, with a deep orange rolled terracotta tile roof, topped at the center and in each corner with magnificent statues. We made our way into the Forum. There were people everywhere. As we climbed the Senate steps, I saw that the assembly had already adjourned for the day. So, we continued to explore more of the city. But soon, we needed rest and started to look for a tavern to eat and get some sleep.

The Senate Curia

Senators of the noble city of Rome, I stand before you, Toscano, emissary of Tressia, with an offer of alliance between our two

262

people, an offer of a long-lasting partnership, one which can be of immense value for both Rome and Tressia. Senators' enemies are easy to come by, and the wars that usually follow can be long and brutal and could bring unbearable costs. The greatest this cost is the loss of the lives of our sons, brothers, and fathers. Wars can have their rewards and glory but inflict much pain and expense. Needless wars are the costliest ones and better avoided. I am here offering Tressia as your ally, an alley that will eliminate the possibility of an unnecessary war between us.

This alliance can save lives, save pain, and gold. Although Tressia has never been an ally of Rome, we have refrained, many times, from becoming your enemy. Most recently evident in your siege of Veii. Tressia did not join in that long, costly war with Rome. We remained neutral. We can remain a neutral neighbor, or we can be something more, your ally and new trading partner. We both have enemies who would like nothing more to see us sacked and ruined. We know our enemies of the past. But the unknown enemy, the one that lies in the future, could be the enemy who does the most unimaginable damage. If we are allies, together we can face the enemies we have now and the enemies of the future. Together we can be prepared to defeat the greatest enemies, those unknown.

Senators, I bring you peace and a new opportunity to prosper. I bring you Tressia, a

new ally. Together we will defeat our
common enemies. Together, we will grow.
Together, we will both be stronger.

Emissary Toscano, you speak well before us
and give us much to consider. Give us time to
think carefully about your offer, and you will
soon have our answer.

Thank you, Senators of Rome. May the gods
guide your deliberations, so we both may
prosper for eternity.

Council Chamber of Tressia

Toscano, we have received a messenger from
Rome. Well done, Commander. The Senate
has agreed to our offer of the alliance. We
now have a thirty-year alliance with Rome.
This is a momentous day for all of Tressia.
We can now live without fear of Rome.

And Rome has gained a great ally in us.

CHAPTER 27: THE SACK OF ROME

The alliance between our two cities enabled Tressia to prosper with abundant, new trading established with Rome. But to our northeast, the Gallic Senones were growing more troublesome. With their numbers expanding, they had outgrown their land in the Po Valley and were looking to expand west over the Apennines. It wasn't long before the situation exploded.

A Tressian noble was traveling back from Arretium when his guards, mistakenly fearing an assault from a band of Gauls foraging nearby, attacked, and killed them. The Senones sent emissaries insisting he was punished and demanded retribution for the killing. The Tressian consul could not agree on a course of action and put the decision before the people of Tressia. The people decided to leave the noble unpunished and that no retribution would be paid. This enraged the Gauls. With little warning, within days, they attacked Tressia, and the city was soon under siege.

The consul decided to send envoys to Rome, asking them to intervene and negotiate with the Gauls. They agreed. Three ambassadors were sent to Gaul's capital city, Medhelanon. They carried the message declaring that Tressia was a friendly city allied with Rome and that Rome would aid them with a force of arms if necessary. They also stated that Rome wished to avoid war and asked the Gauls to clarify what they wanted. The Gallic warlord King Brennus responded that they wished to remain on good terms with the Romans and repeated their claim for retribution for the killing and that it be a substantial portion of land, half of all Tressia. One ambassador asked by what right you must demand such a sizable portion of land from its lawful owners. The king was insulted by the indignant question. He responded that their right is in the points of their swords, and all property belongs to those willing to defend it. The ambassadors quickly concluded the meeting and returned to Rome. The Gauls, enraged, ended their siege of Tressia and gathered their troops for a march on the brazen Rome.

Alerted by reports that the Gauls were rushing toward Rome, the council agreed to send aid to their new ally. I suggested four companies of our most seasoned warriors. The council approved, and we soon headed for Rome. We traveled day and night, making camp, on the third day, ten miles outside the city. By the time we arrived, the battle was

266

already lost. The Gauls were sacking the city. Many parts of Rome were engulfed in flames.

We received reports that a garrison of Romans was making a stand behind fortifications on the heights of Capitoline Hill. We would have to fight through the lines of the entire Gaul army to reach them, and we did not have the force necessary to face them. We returned to our encampment and fortified it, ready to take a stand if the Gauls were to turn and attack us. Not wanting to fight on two fronts, King Brennus of the Senones sent word that he was not interested in attacking us and that his fight was only with the Romans.

They continued to make assaults upon Capitoline Hill, but the fortress was well protected, and the Gauls could not break through the fortifications, so the siege went on unbroken for months.

Both armies ran short on food and were stricken by disease as the months passed. One night, a defender escaped the siege by scaling down the back cliffs and reaching our camp. He told us of this route into the fortress, and we were able to resupply the garrison. This was successful for a brief time, but soon this passage was discovered by the Gauls, and we were forced to stop. Late one night, the Gauls launched an attack using this same approach up the Capitoline cliffs. But again, they were driven back through the heroic combat of one of the veterans in the garrison.

The siege continued. Months later, one of our scouts reported that a Roman General named Furius Camillus, who had retired to the nearby city of Ardea, was gathering scattered Roman soldiers to form an army to liberate the besieged garrison on Capitoline Hill. Many in his army were made up of veterans of his past command. We sent word to him that Tressia was an eager ally wishing to join him. Our forces joined him on the outskirts of La Rustica on his march to Rome. By this time, the Gauls besieging Rome were so weakened by sickness and starvation that they sought a truce. The Gauls agreed to end their siege if a sufficient bounty was paid to them.

We reached the city and entered the Forum unhindered as the negotiations were taking place.

A thousand pounds of gold was agreed to be paid to the Gauls, and a truce was agreed. But as the weighing was done, General Camillus approached the scales and argued that the measurement was unfair, and the agreement fell apart. With our troops fresh and more significant in number, General Camillus told the Gauls to prepare for battle. Ferocious combat ensued there in the Forum. But realizing he was at a disadvantage, King Brennus rallied his men around him and led them outside the city. There he hoped to have space to reorganize them into battle formations.

Outside the City Gates of Rome

General, we would be honored to take the center lines of the formation.

Commander, my detachment will lead the fighting. I was planning to hold your men in reserve.

If I may speak freely, General, your men have only recently been assembled, although exceptional warriors are unfamiliar with each other and not a united force. My men are well-trained and are veterans of many battles together, forming a cohesive fighting force. Let us show you what we can do.

If your men have even half your spirit and courage, they will do well in this battle. The center is yours.

You will not be disappointed, General.

Commander, why aren't your men forming one phalanx?

We form in separate multiple units, General, twenty-one men per unit, seven men across, and three rows deep. Each unit with its commander works tactically together.

That will create gaps in your line where the enemy will charge right through. Your line will be broken, and your units will be crushed.

General, we hold reserve units that remain behind to fill the gaps. It is called maniple formation. It allows for different tactics that can act quickly to changes in battle conditions. Commander Matteo implemented this type of formation for our army years ago. It has been highly influential in battle, allowing flexibility and quick response. We have been extremely formidable using it.

I hope you are right, Commander, the future of Rome depends upon it.

Seeing our unique formation, the Gauls were immediately confused and became unsteady. Sensing their weakness, our men became even more emboldened, and Matteo quickly outmaneuvered their right flank. King Brennus rushed in to stop the side from collapsing, but he was cut down. With their king dead, the Gauls panicked and started to flee. Within an hour, the battle was over, the Gauls completely routed, and the city of Rome liberated.

Rome was ecstatic. With the Senate restored, it bestowed the distinguished honor of "Heroes of Rome" upon Matteo and me for expelling the Gauls in such a dramatic fashion. It also offered Roman citizenship to all Tressians who participated in the battle. In addition, the Senate quickly elected General Camillus as the new Consul of Rome.

The Tressian Camp Outside of Rome

Matteo, the General, was impressed with our multiple-unit formations. He wants his army to learn these tactics. He has asked that you stay in Rome to train his army.

Are we sure we want me to do this, Commander? If we do, you know it will make Rome an even more potent military force than they are now.

Improving Rome's battle tactics will surely add to its dominance on the battlefield. But their dominance is inevitable. With the fall of Veii and now the defeat of the Gauls, Rome's appetite for expansion has undoubtedly increased. The help that we give Rome today will only shorten the time before all of Etruria is enveloped in the growing power of Rome. Tressia is an ally of Rome today, but the day will come when Tressia will be too tempting of a treat for Rome to ignore. I would not have believed this fervor of Rome unless I had experienced it for myself. You can feel it from the General to the Senators to the citizens. They all believe in the future glory of Rome and are eager to sacrifice to make it so. I'm only unsure what part in this we are to play. You should accept the General's offer to stay and train the Roman army. It is essential to learn as much as we can about them. Let the General know I must

271

return to Tressia. He will have my answer on the offer of "Citizenship of Rome" once I have had time to decide fully. You, Matteo, must decide for yourself.

I have already decided this, Commander. Our destiny lies together.

Well then, when you return, we will discuss more where our futures lie.

What of the men, Commander? What should we tell them?

I will speak to them about Rome and its future in the morning.

Men of Tressia, you have won a great battle. You have served Tressia well once again. Your bravery and skill have won the gratitude of our ally, Rome. It has offered citizenship to all of you in return for this victory and for liberating the city. You are free men, and if you wish, you are free to accept this offer and become a citizen of Rome. Men, you are all loyal men of Tressia, a prosperous and honorable city, it is your home, but as free men, you decide where and how you spend your life. This offer is a great honor. Rome has conquered many and harbors unlimited ambitions. Their future is boundless. It is an immense honor to be a Roman and even more significant to be a Roman Etruscan. This decision is yours to make. We are their ally, and they are eager to learn from us. Commander Matteo will stay in Rome to train the Roman army in our unit formations and battle tactics. The Commander is looking for volunteers to aid him with this training. You will be most welcome if you wish to stay and help him. We break camp in an hour for those who want to return to Tressia. The speed of the gods to you all!

CHAPTER 28: THE FUTURE IS ROME

Villa Feonia

Gia, it's so wonderful to hold you in my arms again.

Praise the gods who have brought you back to your son and me. Toscano, these partings are never getting easier. I missed you more than ever.

Yes, I know. I feel it too. Now, who's that tugging at my leg? Is that my son? Is that you, Donato? Look at you! You're a man already! Come up here and let me see how big you've grown.

Toscano, all of Tressia is talking about your victory over the Gauls and how you were honored as a "Hero of Rome." I'm enormously proud of you.

There were many "Heros of Rome." All our men fought bravely that day. I am proud of them all. They have solidified our allegiance with Rome.

And I'm happy that it's over and you are back home, safe with me.

Gia, we need to speak about Rome.

You make it sound serious, Toscano.

Well, I am serious; there is something we need to consider.

Let me bring Donato inside so we can talk.

Gia, the Senate not only honored me as the "Hero of Rome" but also offered us citizenship of Rome.

Well, that is something to be proud of, Toscano, and well deserved.

It is, and we need to consider it seriously.

Citizenship of Rome? We are citizens of Tressia; it is our home. We're well-known, trusted, proud citizens of Tressia. You're its commander. Look at this villa. Why would we want to leave here?

Gia, there is something about that city, something hard to describe. Something that I have not seen or felt before. And it's not just their military power; it's her people. You can feel it. They're destined for greatness, and they are striving for it. It's everywhere, in their philosophy, their attitude, their buildings. What it means to be Roman is unique.

Many here feel the same way about Tressia.

Rome is much different.

What do you mean?

Well, their wars, for example. They are not
fighting to defeat their enemies or for the
destruction of a city. They're after expanding,
annexing territories, and colonizing most of
the cities they conquer. Rome wants more
Romans, many more Romans. That's
uniquely Roman.

Riding into that city for the first time, some of
what we passed reminded me of Tressia.
Only in Rome it's done larger and better. For
hundreds of years, Etruscan kings ruled
Rome. During that time, they have taken
much from us. They are willing learners. And
not just from us. They used the Greeks, the
Egyptians, the Phoenicians, and others,
merging them into Rome. A city with a
resilient spirit and rich culture, built by fierce
loyalty and a strong belief in their eternal
destiny.

That's fine for them. Leave Rome to the
Romans. What is so wrong with Tressia? We
have built our lives here, and we are happy.
Let Rome be as they wish.

But Rome will not let us be, Gia. They'll soon
be right outside our door. It has already
begun, and Etruria has ignored it, hoping
Rome would disappear. We are pretending
that Rome is not a rival, not a threat. We are
not opening our eyes to what is coming, to

what I saw. We have become too complacent, comfortable, spoiled, and satisfied. Many are happy to enjoy our wine, our music, our endless food, our gold jewelry, and fine clothes, having slaves doing the work while they go from banquet to banquet. We are a land no longer willing to sacrifice, grow, or even resolve to protect itself. We are already at the point where we need the help of others to survive, allying with Rome itself. It is only a matter of time before Tressia and all of Etruria are entirely under the dominance of Rome. It has already begun.

Toscano, this doesn't sound like you. I do not know the person who is speaking. Our families, friends, and many others work hard and love Tressia.

Yes, that is true of them, but there are many more in Tressia and the other cities of Etruria who do not live that way. Centuries have passed since most Etruscans lived and felt that way. Our time is fading, now is the time of Rome, and now's the time to be a Roman.

I'm surprised to hear all this; it isn't easy to accept that it is coming from you. I'm astonished that you are convinced about the decline of Tressia and convinced of the future of Rome. I thought you were happy we were together and in this magnificent villa you've earned. You're one of the most respected commanders Tressia has ever had, yet you speak of Rome, the glory of Rome yet to come. It's all hard for me to believe. Is this just you who speaks this way? What of Matteo? He has been to Rome. Does he feel this same way?

He has experienced Rome with his own eyes longer than I. He'll return soon, and we'll see if he still feels as strongly about Rome as I do.

Toscano, I am not sure about any of this, and it would be life-changing for all of us. What about your brother, father, and mother? What will they think and want to do?

We will speak to them, and they'll have to decide for themselves. You and I, we'll decide on this together.

I'm not sure what I feel.

Gia, our lives will be together no matter where we decide to live. I'll only be happy if I'm with you. But I'm thinking not just about us, Gia. I am thinking of Rome for our son, his future, and where he and his family will have a better life. Tressia and all of Etruria, its time has passed. This recent fate with Rome has given us a chance to start a new life in a place that's seizing life. I cannot speak for the rest of our family; it will be for them to decide what is best for them. But I am sure that Rome holds the best future for us.

How can you be so sure?

There is still more to learn about Rome before we make any move, and I want you to feel this same way, Gia. Matteo may help us decide. He's been there for months and will be back soon, and he can tell us what he thinks of Rome and this move.

I'm worried.

Gia, we will not do anything unless we both agree on the future we want for our family.

One Month Later

Matteo, come in. It is good to see you back, my friend.

Glad to be back, Commander.

Come, let's go to the courtyard. There's a cool breeze, and Gia and Vera are waiting there with some wine.

Commander Matteo, it is a pleasure to see you again. You remember my sister, Vera.

Vera, there is no forgetting you. I'm honored. How lovely, both of you.

Matteo, please sit. We are all anxious for you to tell us about your time in Rome, curious about what you've experienced and how you feel about Rome from the time you've spent there.

Rome, well, it is different. But not so different that you'd feel out of place as an Etruscan once you are comfortable speaking in Latin.

What are people like? How different are they from us?

The Romans are ambitious people, always striving to get ahead. Some are overly so, but this competitiveness influences and benefits the city. You can feel a genuine desire for greatness in the streets, the Forum, the many markets, and the army.

That sounds extraordinary.

Like any city, it has problems, but Rome strives for more. They are destined for it, and the Romans will not rest until they achieve it.

Matteo, speaking of the army, how has their training progressed? And what more have you learned about General Camillus?

He is the most ambitious and not afraid to let others know. To celebrate our victory over the Gauls, the Senate hailed him as the "Second Founder of Rome" and presented him with a second triumph. For this, he was undoubtedly flamboyant, parading through the streets riding an elaborate war chariot pulled by a team of four white stallions preceding his army. I have never seen anything like it. He was dressed in a gold-trimmed toga, crowned in laurel, and his face painted bright red, followed by a long procession of captive Gauls.

There were cheering crowds lining the streets leading to the Circus Maximus. Some in the Senate thought this was too pompous of an exhibition and were offended by his lack of humility. But despite this and being a patrician, he proved himself a man of the people. The people love him, and there is no doubt that he is a wise military commander and a clever politician. He insisted his soldiers receive pay for their siege of Veii, endearing himself forever to the entire army. He will remain a dominant force in Rome and on the battlefield for years.

It sounds that way. Tell me about how the training is going.

The Roman army is full of eager learners, both the officers and the men, including the Commander. I have been drilling using our maniple unit formations for months, and there is still much work to be done, but they have acquired the maneuvering and combat skills even faster than the Tressians did when I arrived here.

That's good to hear. You've done well, Matteo. Where have you been staying?

I am staying with the officers on the upper floor of the military barracks above the dormitory, and I have my own space. The building is near the Forum and is quite comfortable. The floors are inlaid with intricate mosaics, and the walls are adorned with military-themed frescos. I am well taken care of, but for you, Commander, I am told by the General himself that if you accept the offer of Roman citizenship and come to Rome, the Senate is ready to appoint you to the position of First-Ranking Centurion. You will have a barrack all to yourself and be paid exceptionally well.

Let's take a break from this talk of Rome.
Come, Matteo, see how Donato and his little
cousin Nico have grown. They are playing
with their toy soldiers in the nursery.

The Bedroom of Villa Feonia

Toscano, wake up! Toscano, you must listen. I
have just spoken to Vera, and we've decided.
We want to move to Rome.

You what?

Vera and I we've decided we want to move to
Rome.

Really?

Yes, it's settled. We want to move to Rome.

Well, then, that is what we will do. Gia, I
promised you that the first thing I want to do
once we are settled there is to have the
wedding.

The Barracks at Villa Feonia

Matteo, are you sure a month will be enough
to find housing in Rome for Vera and my
parents?

A month will be more than enough to find
housing for them. I already know a
neighborhood close to the barracks where
many families of the legionaries live. It's on

the Via Scara. The street is filled with shops, many with second-story bedrooms. Perfect for your father. Many have storefronts and workshops at street level and bedrooms above, large enough for your parents, Vera, and little Nico to live.

And your brother Janus, will he be coming with us to Rome?

He has just finished building out his workshop in Tressia. Once we're settled, he will visit and consider joining us in Rome.

That seems perfect. Safe travels, my friend. If the gods are willing, we will meet in Rome in a month.

Via Scara, Rome

What do you think, father?

Well, it looks like this furnace hasn't been used in years, and this anvil is so rusted that it's useless. And the light back here will be gone by mid-afternoon. Plus, there is hardly enough space here to store my tools, never mind room for the bins I'll need for the ore and slag. And look where I must travel for the water. That fountain is far from here. This will never work.

Well, it sounds perfect, then. We'll take it.

Wait, what? Toscano?

Father, this is the third space we've seen, we have been searching throughout all of Rome, and there are no other places left to look. How many workshops do you think they have available in this city? You'll make this work. This is the one. Plus, look how busy this street is, and with the two large rooms upstairs, there's room for you, mom, Vera, and her baby. So, let's go back to the tavern and get them. I'm sure they would love this space.

Rome's Military Headquarters at Campus Martius

Commander Toscano, it's time you are known by a proper Roman name. With that blond mane of yours, you're now to be known as Toscano Flavius of Rome.

Toscano Flavius of Rome, by appointment of the Senate and I, Marcus Furius Camillus, General of Rome, by the power vested in me, do hereby confer the office and title of First-Ranking Centurion of the First-Ranking Cohort. You are now to swear before Mars your oath of allegiance to Rome.

I, Toscano Flavius of Rome, swear before Mars that I shall faithfully execute all that I am commanded and that I shall never desert my service to Rome, nor shall I seek to avoid death in the name of the Roman Republic.

Congratulations, Centurion.

Thank you, General.

Commander Matteo, you, too, need a proper Roman name. You will now be known as

Matteo Fremitus Lupi, for the wolf's growl
made while you aim your bow.

Matteo Fremitus Lupi of Rome, with the
approval of the Senate of Rome, I, Marcus
Furius Camillus, General of Rome, by the
powers vested in me, do hereby confer onto
you the office and title of Centurion of the
First-Ranking Cohort. You will now swear
your oath to Mars of your allegiance to Rome.

I, Matteo Fremitus Lupi, hereby swear to
Mars that I shall faithfully execute all that I
am commanded and that I shall never desert
my service to Rome, nor shall I seek to avoid
death in the name of the Roman Republic.

Congratulations, Centurion.

Thank you, General.

Legionnaires, you may now salute your new
Centurions.

Now Centurions, come, we barely have time
to celebrate. We must talk. I just returned
from the Curia; the Senate has proclaimed me
Dictator, and we must raise an army. We
have received disturbing news that the
Aequians and Volscians allied troops are in
rebellion. They have marched on Sutrium
and are besieging the city. The Tribune army
encamped near Mount Marcius is close to
being overrun. They're desperate for
reinforcements. We must come to their aid.

General, those legionnaires remaining in the city will barely form half a cohort. Where do we find the men to make this army?

We have no choice. We must put under arms those past the typical age of recruitment. Not even the priests are to be exempt. We will have our army. Centurion, be ready to march by the end of the week.

Streets of Rome

Adrian, look, there are legionnaires going door to door and coming this way.

It's a levy. The Senate is raising a new army.

Indeed, our boys are still too young.

Yes, they are. To be conscripted, you must be at least 18 years, and there is no need to worry. It's me they're after.

Adrian Mercillius?

Yes.

By order of the Senate of Rome, you are hereby conscripted into the legions of Dictator Marcus Furius Camillus. You are to report to Campus Martius tomorrow at noon.

I'll be there, Centurion.

What are the ages of your two sons here, soldier?

My youngest was just fourteen, and Felix, the oldest, will turn 16 in June.

Please, they are just boys, much too young for the army.

Not too young for the Trumpet Corp.

Young Felix, there, have you ever played the flute?

No sir.

What about you? What's your name?

Go ahead. It's fine. Tell the Centurion your name.

My name is Augustus, sir.

Augustus, well, that is a magnificent name. Well, Augustus, have you ever played a musical instrument?

No, sir, I have not.

Well, no matter what, both of you will learn together. Come with your father tomorrow to Campus Martius and report to the Trumpet Corp. Do worry, mother. They will both be well out of danger during their time in the service to Rome and be justly rewarded. Think of it; you will now have two new musicians in your family.

The Countryside Surrounding Mount Marcius

General, our scouts have located the Latin and Tribune camps. They're ten miles to the south, just beyond those mountains ahead.

I see. We'll take this route around and come from behind unnoticed.

General, they've camped a few miles ahead, just over those hills.

As the scouts suggested, we camp on that high ground across the valley. Have the men set the fortifications and light more fires than usual. I want the Aequians, Volscians, and our Tribune to see we've arrived in large numbers.

The Next Morning

General, they are withdrawing from their siege and returning to camp.

Centurion, looking at our position, how would you suggest we proceed?

General, they are reinforcing their defenses, erecting those wooden fortifications on top of the embankments anticipating our attack. With their camp well fortified, a direct assault would require many men and losses to breach, even if we were to plan a surprise attack just before dawn.

So, how do you suggest we defeat them then, Centurion?

We could set fire to their defenses and burn them out, General.

A fire? That's an interesting plan. But it must be a massive fire if it's going to work.

General, if we ram several flaming siege towers into their palisades, the fire will spread to all their fortifications. With the addition of our fire missiles, it will become massive, engulfing their entire camp. It will force them to abandon their positions, escape the blaze, and come out right toward us.

Or the fire may not be large enough to spread and flame out. We need the aid of the winds, Centurion. It needs to push the flames onto their palisades and extend to their fortifications, engulfing their entire encampment. The winds usually blow down the mountains from the east in the mornings, right towards their camp. That's where we'll send our siege towers, attacking their east embankment. If the winds blow hard, your plan might work.

Centurion, prepare the fire missiles and the towers. If the gods approve, the winds will blow strong and steady tomorrow, and we shall burn them out as you say. We will attack tomorrow as soon as we have our winds.

General, there's still no wind.

Be patient, Commander. It's still early. Let the sun do its job and heat the valley. The warm air will rise and draw the cooler air from the mountains. It shouldn't be much longer.

General, look, our banners are starting to flap in the wind.

Centurion, the gods favor us. Sound the horns and make ready to attack.

We are in position, General.

Light the towers and give the order to move them forward. When inflamed, move them to the edge of their trenches and topple them onto the barrier.

Yes, General.

Now, fire the missiles.

Archers ready! Fire!

Commander, the far tower, the fire is going out. They're drowning out the flames.

Matteo, have the fire archers concentrate on top of that last tower, and we need it to stay afire.

It's not working, Commander; it is soaking with water.

Matteo, fill your water pouch with the oil and grab that torch. Ride with me. We're going to keep that tower afire.

Matteo! Matteo! Leave your mount; he's too injured. Grab the torch and hop on. We'll ride together.

Hand me the pouch, Matteo, now pass me the torch.

It's lit, Commander. It's working; the whole tower is ablaze.

Grab my hand. Let's go.

The fire is starting to engulf the entire camp. Give the order for the men cut down anyone trying to escape.

Legionnaires! Follow me!

Well done, Commander.

Thank you, General.

Look, a little late, but here comes the Tribune army. Escort the Tribune to my tent. We will plan the attacks on Aequi and Volsci and then on to Sutrium to liberate them.

Military Barracks of Rome

Matteo, what do you think about these Roman shields?

Commander, they offer little protection in close combat from slashes of heavy swords and even less protection from missile fire.

I agree. The Etruscan long shields are far superior, and we must demonstrate that to the General and convince him to make a change. My father brought some with him. Let's show them first to our men and see how they react.

Military Courtyard

You two legionnaires, hand me your shields. Now each of you, take one of these and get ready to defend yourselves. Now you two over there, take these swords and strike at them. Use your full strength. Start again. Defenders, use your shield to fend them off. This time all of you make me believe it's real.

Legionnaires, in a missile attack, what would you do?

How did you get the idea to shield the head of the legionnaire in front of you?

It seemed natural, Commander. These shields are curved, so you can still see under them when it's over your head. They reminded me of the shell of a pet testudo I once had as a child.

What is your name, legionnaire?

Claudius, Commander.

Claudius, if you had a choice, which shields would you carry into battle?

These long-curved ones, Commander.

Military Barracks

Claudius, tell us about the pet testudo you had while growing up.

Commander, must I?

It would help if you told us about it, Claudius. Go ahead, don't be shy; we all want to hear.

Well, there was a small pond near where I lived when I was young. I would go there to catch baby testudos. On suitable mornings, I could see them by the handful. Some of my friends would come, and they would bring them back home to make soup.

One summer, I caught a full-grown one. It was so large that I decided to bring it home and keep it as a pet. My mother wouldn't allow me to bring it into the house. So, I drilled a small hole in the back of its shell, attached it to a long cord, and fastened it to a stake planted in the field behind our home.

I would go out in the mornings and pull it out of the tall grasses, where it would be hiding, feeding it. After a while, it started to eat right out of my hand. Early one morning, I was awakened by loud squealing from the field. As I got close, there was just enough light to see a group of ferrets attacking my testudo. They had him surrounded. His head and tail were tucked beneath his protective shell, and he had dug his claws deep into the grass, gripping tightly to the ground. They were scratching and biting at him, trying to turn him over, but they couldn't grasp him. One of the ferrets then bit on the cord, tugging and yanking at it, trying to pull him loose. I snatched a stick and swung it widely at them. Finally, they gave up and ran off. I could see their bite marks all over the edge of his shell.

He stayed there, not moving for days, with his head and feet tucked under his shell. He wouldn't even poke his head out to eat the pieces of lettuce I left right in front of him. After over a week, finally, I saw him moving.

He started scraping the ground behind him with his claws, tugging the cord, trying to free himself. Seeing how desperate he was to escape, I felt he had earned his freedom, and I cut the cord, freeing him. He meandered off into the tall grass, heading toward the pond. I returned to that pond all through my childhood but never saw him again. To this day, I hope he still lives and has remained free.

That is quite a story, Claudius. In honor of Claudius's pet testudo, our shield formation will officially be called the "Claudius Testudo." Let us give a toast to Claudius's heroic pet testudo. "Centum Annos!"

Centum Annos!

See, Claudius, your testudo will live on forever!

Via Scara

Toscano, come down to the workshop, Matteo and I have something we want to show.

I'll be right back, Mother. Keep the Isicia Amulata warm for me

I will. When you get downstairs, please tell your father that his dinner is ready.

Now, what've you two been up to down here?

Over here, look at this!

It looks fearsome. What is it?

A Ballista.

A Ballista? What can it do? You must show me.

First, you place a long arrow in this slot and then use this lever to crank back this slide. You adjust the aim here like this, and once it's all set, you stand back and pull on this cord, releasing the trigger, and it fires.

The two of you were able to make this weapon?

It was mainly your father. I showed him my miniature version, and he scaled it to full size. We've been working on it since we arrived in Rome, and it's been revised over ten times to get the power we needed. Wouldn't you say so, Lucien?

At least that many.

Remarkable. Let me look at your miniature. I have never seen anything like this before. Where did you get it?

I've had it since I was a boy, growing up in Vacalvi. Do you remember that story I told you about that old bower who made my first hunting bows?

Yes, we were all sitting around that campfire roasting the roebuck I had just killed when we first met.

If I remember correctly, Toscano, there was some dispute on which strike brought down that roebuck.

Yes, there was, but it was resolved quickly, thanks to Nico.

It was a joint effort.

Well, put, Matteo. Now go ahead and tell us where you got this miniature "Ballista," you called it.

Growing up, I always enjoyed going to this bowers workshop after our training was done for the day. The craftsman was named Nerie, Nerie Cala. He was highly skilled and one of the best woodworkers I have ever seen. His shop was crammed with so many tools and supplies that there was hardly any space for his workbench. He had bundles of wood, separated by species, with heaps of strings, piles of feathers, and stacks of arrows and bows in various stages of completion. He loved to tell me stories about his youth and how he learned to hone his craft while I watched him work. He had no sons, so when we first met, he hoped I would become his apprentice.

On one of my visits, I arrived before he wasn't there. So, I started to look around. There was so much to explore in every nook and cranny. This strange-looking object was in one dark corner in the back of his shop, sitting on a high shelf. I climbed up on a stool to reach it and bring it into the light to get a closer look. I heard his voice behind me saying, *"Be careful with that. It's not a toy."* It was this miniature Ballista. We sat for hours as he told me how he got it.

He spoke about where he was born and how he was an apprentice for his father, Theo, starting even younger than I was. He said he grew up in Siracusa, the Greek colony on Sicily. There, his father was a master woodworker, known to be the most highly skilled in all the colony. One day an inventor named Phidias came into his father's shop with a drawing for a strange new weapon he had designed. He asked my father if he thought he could make it. He looked, and before long, he said he could. After many months he was finally able to construct a full-sized working Ballista. Phidias showed it to a Syracusian army officer he knew. And soon, his father was commissioned to produce a more powerful version for the army.

A brief time later, the city came under siege by the Athenians. They say the invaders were repelled primarily due to this powerful new long-range weapon. The famous general of Syracuse, General Dionysius, himself honored his father and the inventor with a handsome reward.

A few years later, there were three different wars with the Carthaginians, and by this time, they were building hundreds of Ballistae, and Syracuse had become known as the best-fortified city in all of Greece.

His father became a wealthy man and took Nerie on a journey to the Greek colony of Cumae on the mainland. He said his father needed a rest from all the demands of building more powerful Ballistae. In Cumae, his father had a spacious villa overlooking the Tyrrhenian Sea. They both lived there comfortably for a brief time before his father became ill and died. Alone and still only 12 years of age, all that was left to him was lost. He was taken in by his housekeeper, Petrui, an Etruscan slave whom his father freed shortly before his death on the condition that she would become the boy's guardian. His new guardian took him back with her to her home in Tressia. Nerie took this miniature Ballista his father had given with him when he left. He stayed with his guardian Petrui, never marrying until she died.

With the woodworking skills his father had taught him, he had opened a bow-making shop in the city. Years later, I asked him why he never built a working scale in Tressia to become rich like his father. He told me he tried, but the work only brought back too many sad memories of his father and was too painful for him to continue.

On one of my last visits, knowing that we might not be together again, the old man gave the miniature to me. He said it might be helpful to me one day, and I've kept it with me ever since.

Rome's Military Headquarters

Centurion, come in. What is on your mind?

Our armaments, General, if I may.

Indeed, speak freely, Centurion.

First, I would like to speak with you about a long-range missile weapon.

I'm listening.

Well, it's easier if I show it to you. General, look at this.

What is this?

It's a miniature of a mechanical missile launching weapon. Matteo has had it since he was a boy. It can fire large missiles accurately over a great distance. It's called a Ballista, developed first by the Syracusans. They have successfully used full-scale models in battles for a long while.

How far can it reach?

It is accurate for up to three hundred yards, General. The furthest distance it can reach is close to five hundred yards.

How did he get it?

It was a gift from an old craftsman from Syracuse he knew as a boy.

Can we find an artisan in Rome who can make a working model?

Yes, General, I know of one already. My father, Lucien, and Matteo have already constructed one.

I should have known. When can I see it, Centurion?

Now, General. It's set up and waiting for you in the Circus Maximus. That's the closest location with enough open space for a demonstration.

That's fine, let's go. Guards, have my horse readied and bring up a mare for the Centurion.

Circus Maximus

You must be Lucine. It's a pleasure. You must be immensely proud of your son.

I am General. I have been proud of him ever since he was a boy.

You have the right to be so. He has also impressed me on many occasions. Now Matteo, tell me more about how you came across this model.

I obtained it in my youth from a craftsman, General. It was given to him by his father, who passed it down to me. I was told the working models were instrumental in defending Syracuse. I showed it to Lucien soon after we arrived here in Rome. In a few months, he made this full-scale version. He had revised it many times before he succeeded in constructing a functional military weapon.

Well, it certainly looks impressive. Let's see what it can do.

General, that first target is set at three hundred yards, and that further, larger one, is at four hundred yards.

That was very convincing. Well done, Lucien. Well done to all of you.

Centurion, get this to the military workshop and have them begin making more of these. Lucien, if you don't mind, I would like you to review the details with them on how this was made. Wait, Lucien, what is this metal being used here?

It's iron, General.

Iron? Another mystery from Etruria. Tell me more about this iron, Lucien.

Before we left Tressia, I was outfitting the army with weapons and armaments made of iron. We added it to shields to make breastplates and even swords. It is much more complicated than copper or even bronze. Swords and daggers made of iron are stronger and sharper, and iron breastplates are more flexible and lighter yet offer better protection than chainmail.

The Tressian army uses this iron now?

It has begun to, and it is spreading to other Etruscan cities as well. The Greeks and Carthaginians have been using iron weapons for years. It was first discovered in East Asia decades ago, but only recently has knowledge of this metal begun to spread here.

Where are the Tressians getting this metal?

It was first mined on Elba, but it can be found in many places. The ore is usually mined where copper is found, and it's abundant and can be found right here in the hills surrounding Rome. But it needs to be smelted differently.

How did you learn all of this?

On Elba. I've smelt it there. It's an involved process, and only an experienced blacksmith familiar with the ore has the knowledge and skill to do it correctly. It can even be refined even further into something called steel.

Steel?

Yes, General, and an even more refined form of iron. It is more durable than ordinary iron when forged correctly. With the right skills, it can be made into an exceptional sword.

And you have such skills, Lucien?

Some say I do.

He is being modest, General. I can attest that he indeed does. My father was known to be one of the most talented blacksmiths in Etruria and has worked with metals all his life.

Lucien, tell me more about yourself and how you first came across this iron.

I come from a lengthy line of blacksmiths, working with copper, bronze, tin, and even silver for many years. I honed my trade early, apprenticing for the most skilled blacksmiths in Etruria. But knowledge of working this iron ore has only recently become known here. I learned to smelt while working at a copper mining camp on Elba. It's truly a valuable metal. It has properties far beyond all previously known metals. It can be forged into powerful weapons, holding a sharp edge yet not brittle. Far superior to copper or even bronze. It can also make durable, solid, and long-lasting tools for tradespeople and farmers. Its uses are sweeping, General.

How many shields and swords have you made with this iron already?

Enough to outfit over fifty men, General.

Do you have any of these items with you here in Rome?

In my workshop, I have two Etruscan shields edged with iron and a long sword made of steel. I can bring them to you if you wish, General.

Yes, I would very much like to see them. Today, Lucien, if possible.

The Military Courtyard

A shield of this size, one would think, would be much heavier and too burdensome to wield in battle. But it doesn't seem heavier than my Roman round shield.

Its weight has been lessened by gluing three thin planks of wood together instead of using one thick plank.

But is it still strong enough not to break apart when hit by a javelin or a heavy blow from an ax?

It is extreme and durable, General. The panels are glued together with their grains crossed, giving them great strength and flexibility. Even a well-thrown javelin will not break it apart. And this round protruding iron center strengthens it further to be used as a punching and thrashing weapon in close combat.

Attractive, and this metal cladding along the top edge looks like the iron used in constructing your Ballista.

The iron cladding at the top edge protects it from powerful thrashing blows.

Go ahead, General, take your gladius and see what damage you can do to it.

I've done more damage to my sword than I have done to this shield. How quickly can you make ten of these long shields and gladiuses made with this iron, Lucien? I would like to see how they perform in actual combat.

If I had the iron ore and the wood planks on hand, and with the aid of an assistant or two, I should be able to make ten of these shields and ten iron gladiuses in a week.

I will make sure you have what you need. Now, tell me more about this steel sword of yours.

Iron ore smelting must be done with fire much hotter than the average temperature for smelting copper or bronze. To get the fire that hot, the flames need to be enhanced by using bellows, forcing air streams onto the coals. When the flames become white-hot, you know your fire is at the desired temperature. The iron is then drawn out of the ore and forms a bloom at the bottom of the furnace. The bloom is cooled in water, hammered, and folded many times to forge it into a blade. Finally, the edges are ground sharp, and the blade is highly polished to produce a steel sword of this quality. The process is exacting, requiring expert smelting, and forging skills to get it right,

General. If not done correctly, the steel will be too brittle, and cracks will form, making the sword useless.

This has all been most enlightening, Lucien. You are a highly skilled and talented blacksmith, and your knowledge and skills will be most appreciated. Thank you for sharing them.

Thank you, General. I'm glad I can help.

Military Headquarters

Toscano, how quickly can you obtain the iron ore and wooden planks for your father to make these new shields and swords?

I'm sure I can find all the iron ore and lumber he needs in Tressia, and I could be there and back here in a week.

The Quartermaster will give you all the coins you need. Take your father, the men, and the supplies you need, and be back in Rome as soon as possible.

Lucien's Workshop

Father, are you ready to leave?

One moment Centurion, let your mother finish packing our food for the journey.

Father, the wagon is already full of supplies, and the men are waiting. We must leave.

I'm coming, but I'm a little too old to live on those provisions your army supplies.

So, what is mother packing for you?

It's for you and the men, her famous Isicia Amulata.

Of course, now let's go. Hold on, father, it's going to be a bumpy ride.

Have you ever thought about the friends you left in Tressia?

I've been too busy to think about Tressia. Plus, with you, Gia, and Donato all here in Rome, there is nothing in Tressia that's important to me. Are you happy to be in Rome, Centurion?

I am. And eager about my new command under General Camillus.

So, you are happy with your life as a soldier, fighting wars?

War is a grueling and dangerous profession, father. But I feel I'm where I'm supposed to be, doing what I do best.

You haven't changed, Toscano. You speak the same as you did when you were a boy.

It was true then, father, and still is true today. And I have you to thank for helping to make my wishes happen. Where do you think we should head, for the mines at Colline Metallifere or your old workshop in the city?

There is no telling what we'll find at my old workshop. That blacksmith I sold it to was more interested in bronze work than smelting ore. We should head straight to the mines. With all the smelting going on, we will find an ample supply of iron nuggets to buy and bring back to Rome.

Lucien's Workshop

Does this gladius feel balanced to you, Toscano?

Father, you've worked on it for hours. It feels fine. I'll put it in the wagon with the others. Now let's go. The General is anxious to see us.

Military Courtyard

Toscano, are you ready for the mock combat demonstration?

General, these shields and swords are quite different from the ones the men are accustomed to using. They need more time to prepare before engaging in a proper demonstration.

How much time, Centurion?

They'll be ready by the morning, General.

Granted, 'till morning then.

General, the first demonstration will be to assess the Etruscan long shields against a bronze gladius in mock combat.

Company! Battle formation!

Legionnaires, remember the General needs to see a realistic combat engagement. Use all your strength striking your blows onto those long shields.

Legionnaires, Ready! Charge!

General, now to show the shields under missile fire.

Attention company! Form the Testudo!

Archers! Ready! Fire!

Javelins! Ready! Fire!

Impressive, Centurion. Who devised that formation? What did you call it? The Testudo?

Yes, one of the men did, General. His name is Claudius. He got the idea from watching his pet testudo defending itself against an attack of ferrets when he was a boy.

Interesting, bring him to me. Inspiration like that should be rewarded. And Centurion, I want to see how these shields and iron gladius do in a vigorous battle engagement.

Have half a cohort outfitted with these new
shields and iron gladius and ready for
maneuvers in a month? And as for that
Ballista machine, we will need ten more of
them produced. I want to be certain that all
these armaments perform well together in
active combat before we commit to outfitting
our entire army.

Half the cohort? In a month?

Yes, a month, Centurion. The quaestor will
aid you in securing all that is needed. Oh,
Centurion, congratulate your father for me
on those shields, gladius, and that Ballista
machine. They all performed exceedingly
well. If it continues, he and you will have
guided the restructuring of our entire army.

Thank you, General, I will tell him.

The Military Barracks

Men, the General was impressed; he wanted
to expand the combat testing to half a cohort.

Commander, there is a messenger out front
asking for you.

Send him in.

Centurion Toscano?

Yes, I am he.

The General asks if you wouldn't mind
joining him at his residence.

When?

Right now, Centurion.

Certainly, you lead the way.

The Palatine Hill

We first passed by the Circus Maximus to
reach the General's villa. Then after traveling
many more blocks, we continued through the
securely guarded Palatine gates, entering a
secluded section of the city. I had never seen
this part of the city before. As we followed
the road up the Palatine hill, the villas on
either side were striking. The further we
ascended, the more elaborate they became.
By now, many were immense palaces, set far
back from the road, with lavish pathways
lined with tall lean cypresses and sculpture
plantings leading to their entrances. It was all
very imposing.

This way, Commander.

Centurion, thank you for coming on such
short notice. Please come in. Let's go out to
the gardens. Many of the plantings are in full
bloom this time of year.

It is quite beautiful, General.

It is. It's been my home for over ten years,
first given to me following my victory over
the city of Veii. But that's about to change,
and I invited you here, Toscano. The Senate is

313

honoring me with another Triumph for our conquest over the Latins and Volscians. Although I am incredibly grateful for this honor, I have refused to accept it. So instead of another Triumph, the Senate has offered me a new villa, the villa of Romulus.

Congratulations General! That is certainly a high honor. And one that you've earned.

Centurion, your valuable service to Rome deserves to be recognized, and the Senate has agreed. Toscano, in honor of your service, Rome is presenting you with this residence. Look around, Toscano. Where we are standing right now is all yours.

I'm speechless, General.

You need not say anything, Toscano. No one in all of Rome deserves to live here now more than you. The battles we have fought together in the name of Rome were not won by me alone. You, Centurion, have contributed to help secure these victories, and now all of Rome will know the magnitude of what you have done.

Guards, please show Centurion Toscano the rest of his new home. You must excuse me, and I must take my leave. The Senate calls once more.

General, I am profoundly grateful, and it is an honor to serve you.

CHAPTER 31: ROME IS OUR HOME

I'm astonished. I've never seen anything as magnificent. Toscano, your general, and the Senate must profoundly believe in you.

They must. Now come, let me show you the inside.

There are enough rooms here for our whole family to join us.

There are more than enough, plus servants. Come, you must see the gardens. They overlook the entire city.

Toscano, this is breathtaking. It's hard to believe this is going to be our home. There is so much space, and so full of light. We must give it a name, a fitting Roman name. Let me think for a moment. How do the Romans say sunshine?

Solaris, I believe.

Villa Solaris, how does that sound? The Sunshine Villa.

It sounds like our new home. And the perfect setting for something I have been promising for a while; our wedding.

Our wedding?

Yes, now you will finally have it, here at our new home, Villa Solaris.

Oh, my gods, this is so wonderful.

Military Training Grounds at Campus Martius

General, may I have a word?

Yes, of course, come in. What's on your mind, Centurion?

General, I would like to present two further options for our armaments for you to consider.

I'm listening, Centurion.

As you know, these barbarians have always relied on their powerful slashing with heavy swords in close combat, smashing shields, and battering their enemies with blows to the head and shoulders to win battles. With our shields now clad in iron, their blows will be blunted, and their swords bent or shattered. But our bronze helmets, General, still offer little protection and are often crushed by these impacts.

Go on.

If our legionaries wore helmets also forged of iron, these blows would glance off and inflict far less damage. That would be especially true when their hair is raveled under their helmets, cushioning the impact and deflecting the blows onto the shoulder plating.

Sounds wise, Centurion. Let me see such a helmet in combat. It will be done if I am convinced it responds as you describe.

Thank you, General. The second proposal concerns modifying one of our weapons. Our soldiers are skilled at using their javelins as missiles and launching them at the enemy, striking our enemies and disabling their shields. But what if they also carried a second, longer, heavier spear fashioned with an iron blade and the shaft made of ash? It could be used in close, hand-to-hand combat as a stabbing weapon, out of range of the Gaul's heavy swords, and driven into them under their shields while our men would remain safe from the barbarian's heavy swords.

Interesting, Centurion. It could be an especially useful armament but would require specialized training to be used effectively. Have a company outfitted as you describe and supply the training. Centurion, this must be done quickly; if we are ready to put it to use against the Gauls. They will be upon us again soon.

Training Grounds at Campus Martius

You Senones, you are bloodthirsty barbarians and, on my order, will fiercely attack those Romans in formation over there. You're to charge them on the sound of the trumpets, screaming, half-naked, terrifying your enemy. You'll not be satisfied until all those Romans die or beg for mercy. Senones, let me hear you, your best savage screaming.

Haaaaaaa!

Louder!

HAAAAAAAA!!

 Legionnaires, ready spears!

Trumpeters sound the attack.

Centurion, that was embarrassing. Their spears are much too easily separated. The men must remain, shoulder to shoulder, disciplined and tightly formed. Start again.

No, some on the flank are still becoming separated. They must remain tightly formed and strike with much greater force. They will be slaughtered unless they get this right. Again.

Yes, Centurion.

Better, but there is one more element they need to complete their training. Have the company reform here, in front of me.

318

Legionnaires, do you see and hear those warriors on the other end of the field? Don't just look at them. See what they are trying to do. They're trying to strike fear into you and make you doubt yourself, your training, your resolve, your discipline, and your faith in the man beside you. They're trying to ready you to break and run, so they can hunt you down alone and slaughter you one by one. It can only happen if you let them. They're barbarians. They must not break you. They must not break the discipline of a single Roman. You will not let them. The man beside you is ready to fight for you, for Rome. You are together as one, Roman with Roman. Together, you will be the ones who strike fear into them. Together you will cut them down. You are Roman! Mars Ultor!

Mars Ultor! Mars Ultor! Mars Ultor!

Centurion, now they are ready. Sound the attack.

CHAPTER 32: THE WEDDINGS

Villa Solaris

Toscano, you must come. Vera and Matteo are in the courtyard and have something to ask us.

It seems like you already know what it is.

Yes, I do. But come, find out for yourself.

Vera, Matteo, here he is.

So, I hear you have something you'd like to ask me.

Well, we do, to both of you.

Go ahead before Gia bursts out right in front of all of us.

Tuscano, and Gia, we ask you both for your blessing to be married.

Oh, my gods! This is so wonderful. I'm glad for both of you!

320

So, Gia, do they have your blessing?

Yes! Oh, my gods, yes! Yes, you have my blessing.

As for me, it's also a yes. You have my blessing.

This is so wonderful. Vera, oh my gods, when? When will it be? Have you picked a date?

We haven't, but we'd like it to be soon. I long to have Matteo as my husband and little Nico wants him as badly as his father.

And he shall have a great one in Matteo.

Thank you, Toscano. Thanks to both of you. It's important to us that you both approve, and we have your blessings.

Of course, my friend, there's no doubt you two will make a great couple. Gia, come, let's leave these two for a moment. I have something I would like to discuss with you. Please excuse us, just for a moment. Gia, what do you think of inviting them to be married here, at Villa Solaris?

Yes, what an excellent idea, it will be so beautiful here.

Oh, one more thing, what about making it a double wedding, ours and theirs, right here at Solaris, together?

Oh, my gods, our wedding also?

Yes, it's long overdue. You must pick a date. I must formally have you as my wife.

Oh, yes, Toscano, that will be amazing, sisters, both married here together, how perfect.

Are you sure, Gia? We could have separate ceremonies if you wish.

No, no, my sister, we will be married together. I'm so excited. Let's see what they think.

Yes! Oh, my gods, yes, a double wedding, both of us married together, here in the glorious villa. How wonderful, that is so kind of both of you.

Come, Vera, let's do some planning right now. It's going to be so special.

Congratulations, Matteo. Vera is strong-willed and will make a brilliant wife.

Yes, she will. Thank you again for doing all this, Commander. It means a lot to us.

Matteo, no friend means more to me than you, or should I now say, my brother.

Now, actual brothers. I knew that day we met in the Lemon Forest that we were destined to be brothers.

I felt that same way. Destiny has brought us together and is keeping us that way. Now, brother, let's talk about what we must do together. I have some tactics I am considering using with the new weapons that we need to discuss.

Yes, Commander.

The two of you, no more of that army talk, Vera and I have picked a date for our wedding. It must be June to honor Juno and secure her blessings. How is the Ide of June for both of you?

It is fine with me. Matteo?

Yes, the Ide of June will be perfect. I cannot wait much longer to have Vera as my bride.

It is done, then. Our weddings will be held together in June. Here at Villa Solaris. It will be so wonderful. Now we must talk about whom you would wish to invite. It can be as many as you two would like. This villa has enough space for a great many.

Via Scara, Rome

Your gown fits beautifully, Vera. Hold still so I can tie this belt around your waist. There, it is done.

How did you tie that?

With the traditional wedding knot of Hercules. Nothing will be able to pull you two apart now.

How wonderful. Thank you, mother, thank you for everything. I had no idea you knew all about any of these Roman customs.

Of course, I've been hoping this day would come. Here's your veil. Let's try it on and see how you look.

Oh, my gods, Vera, you look breathtaking.

Come, Gia, it's your turn. Let me start braiding your hair. There, how do you like it?

Oh, it's perfect, mother, thank you.

Let's put on your gowns. Look at both of you; how wonderful. You both look so beautiful. I have two lovely young daughters.

You do. You are the mother of both brides.

Oh, my gods, they're coming! I can see the priest leading Toscano and Matteo, and a whole procession is following. Quick, let's go downstairs.

Vera, Gia, remember, you must act frightened and protest loudly. Your husbands are abducting you, it's tradition, and it will help keep the evil omens from ruining your happy marriage.

I won't be acting; it all does sound frightening.

You have nothing to be frightened about, my child; it's going to be a beautiful wedding for the both of you. Now, get ready. Here they come.

No, leave me alone, stop, put me down, stop. No! Help! Stop, leave me alone.

Help, save me! Help! Help me!

Come, don't give me such trouble, women. You are mine.

Let go of me! I will not come with you.

You are. You're coming with me.

Very convincing. Now, let us all leave and follow them in a procession. First, you, Lucien, as the father of both the grooms, you're to lead the procession back to the villa. Then Eugenia, the bride's mother, you're next, along with the children. Then I will follow, leading the choir, musicians, and the rest of the procession.

Come, Donato and Nico, come quick, hold my hands.

Matteo, Tuscano, you may put down your brides. Now, the two couples continue walking, hand in hand, the rest of the way, the brides on your left. You now begin your life's journey together.

Vera, you look beautiful. I love you.

I am so happy to be marrying you, Matteo. I'll love you forever.

Matteo, you first take a piece of this loaf, pull it apart, and scatter the pieces over your lover's head. Now you, Toscano, you do the same to Gia. It will implore the goddess Juno to bestow her blessing upon the brides.

Now everyone, take pieces of the bread and toss them over the couples, ensuring the goddess will bless their union.

Matteo, now you are to pick up your bride and carry her over the threshold. You are signifying you're ready to start your new beginning together.

Now it's your turn Toscano, pick up your bride and carry her over the threshold.

Good, now everyone, we follow them to the tapestry in the garden. There, we witness them exchanging their marriage vows.

Each couple, join your right hands and face each other, and all of you repeat, after me, *"Wherever you shall go, I shall go with you."*

"Wherever you shall go, I shall go with you."

Again, now louder, everyone, and let the singing and music begin.

"Wherever you shall go. I shall go with you."

Again, say it loudly, so our goddess Juno and everyone here can hear you proclaim your marriage vow.

"Wherever you shall go, I shall go with you."

Matteo, Toscano, you may now kiss your bride.

It is time for bridesmaids to lead married couples to their beds, so they can forever seal their union.

Toscano, it was a magnificent feast and such a charming ceremony. This villa has never hosted such a joyous occasion.

Thank you, General. I am glad you enjoyed the festivities. We're happy we were able to have it here. It has made everything that much more captivating.

Toscano, today is a day of much joy. Thank you for inviting me. But I must speak to you privately for a few moments before I leave. There's an urgent business that we must discuss.

Certainly, General.

CHAPTER 33: UNREST IN ROME

Atrium of the Villa Solaris

Toscano, news has come to the Senate that
the Gauls are terrorizing the northern
countryside. Refugees escaping the carnage
are pouring into the city. Remembering the
past horrors inflicted by the Gauls in the
sacking of Rome, they're planning to name
me Dictator again and to mobilize an army to
defeat them.

There will be much dissent among ordinary
people when this news is spread. Much of it, I
expect, will be stirred by Marcus Manlius
Capitolinus. He feels he is now more
deserving of this position than I am. He
harbors much jealousy towards me and has
fashioned himself ahead of me as a man of
the people. He has been recently courting
sympathetic plebeian members of the Senate
for their backing. I'm afraid some are now
calling him *"The Father of the Commons."*

But others feel he has gone too far with his talk and has been rallying the people against the Senate. Some have said he had incited them to riot and storm the Senate to force them into naming him as dictator. It is treasonous behavior, and we must stop him.

What do you propose, General?

After I take my leave, I would like you to start a conversation with one of your guests here, Senator Gaius Lulius. He is held in high regard among the Comitia Curiata and has a large following. He has been sympathetic to our cause in the past. Let him let you know that you have heard in the ranks of this traitorous talk against the Senate being spread by Manlius. And I feel that I shouldn't be named dictator at this time. Suggest to him that I would rather have Quintus Capitolinus be made Dictator in my place. He is willing and in a better position to end the unrest of the people and this treasonous talk than I. As Dictator, he can imprison Manlius and expose him as a traitor. I have already mentioned these intentions to my old commander, Senator Lucius Papirius, and he will play his part also in getting this done.

Your abilities in politics, General, are only surpassed by your skills on the battlefield.

To survive in Rome, Toscano, you must recognize that your battles are everywhere and never truly over. Now go and remember that wisdom. It will apply to you one day soon.

The Curia Hostilia: Quintus Capitolinus, Presiding

Marcus Manlius, you have been seen making false and defamatory accusations of embezzlement of public money by the Senate and inciting rioting among the citizenry with calls of sedition. The Senate has found you a tyrant of Rome and guilty of treason, condemning you to serve five years in prison.

As news of this ruling began to spread throughout the city, crowds soon appeared and started storming the Senate building. The rioting soon spread to other portions of the city, as well. The following day, the Senate reconvened in an emergency session and succumbed to the wishes of the mobs. Quintus ordered Manlius' sentence suspended and had him released.

Now freed and even more encouraged, Manlius soon renewed his accusations against the Senate, inciting outright rebellion among the masses. The Senate had no choice but to quickly appoint Camillus as a military tribune to restore order and put Manlius back on trial.

The Rostra

Senators, citizens, my fellow Romans, turn now and look behind you to the crest of the Capitoline Hill. Now, with your eyes fixed, remember the battle fought not long ago to save all of Rome. Many good men, my friends, your sons, and brothers, died on that hill, giving their lives for the glory of Rome. I stood with them, captain of the guards, fighting to the death for Rome, fighting for your freedom. Many were your sons. They are gone, died there, no longer here to celebrate the freeing of Rome with you. Yet this freedom, earned by their blood, still has not been fairly given to many of us. Judge me for my actions and praise Mars that I am here with you. I am here by his power to free the ordinary people of Rome. Someday, with his blessings, all of Rome will taste this freedom! Vivat Roma! Vivat Roma!

Vivat Roma! Vivat Roma! Vivat Roma!

The speech moved the people and the Senatorial judges, and the raucous reaction of the crowd in the Forum made it impossible to pass a verdict on Manlius. Sensibly, Camillus adjourned the proceedings and scheduled them for the following day. He wisely transferred the trial location to the Patelline Grove, out of sight of Capitoline Hill. The charges were again raised against Manlius by the judges, this time with great fervor, and now a new decision and a bitter new sentence were passed.

Manlius was convicted of treason and condemned to death. The conviction was fittingly conducted at the Tarpeian Rock. Those same cliffs on the far side of Capitoline Hill where he had once fought bravely to save Rome. But now, it was the very place where he was hurled to his death.

Heading North Towards Antemnae

General, our scouts have found the Gauls. They're encamped in the Anio Valley. The scouting reports number their strength at over fifteen thousand.

That's hard to believe. The Gauls have never been able to raise an army of that size.

The barbarian army includes Greek axillary and mercenary units from all over Etruria.

Come, Centurion, we must see this for ourselves.

Valley of Anio

Centurion, what do you see?

The scouting reports seem correct, General. They're at least fifteen thousand strong, supplemented by those mercenary units.

What mercenaries do you see?

332

The Greek hoplite troops in the center, plus those on the flanks, look like Samnites and Volscians mercenary units.

Look closely. Who else do you see on that far flank?

Etruscans, General.

Yes, Etruscans, Toscano. It's tomorrow then that you must kill Etruscans. Are you a faithful Roman, ready to kill or be killed, no matter who the enemy is, Centurion?

I am Roman, and I'm ready, General.

Good, that is what I expect of you. Now, look towards their camp. What do you see there in the middle?

I see booty, General, stolen from the surrounding farms and villages.

They're gorging themselves on our food and wine, even though they know we are close. And what of their fortifications?

There are none, General.

Exactly, they're overconfident, bolstered by their considerable numbers. They don't see us as a real danger. They're more interested in feasting instead of preparing for battle. Now that we know what we will face, I want our numbers hidden. Set the most significant part of our forces down in those hollows, fenced-in behind trenches. Have them lying quietly, out of sight. Take four cohorts and set camp up on that hill in plain view. I want to give them the impression that those cohorts form our entire force. We attack tomorrow, just before dawn, catching them sleeping off their feast. Our new ballistae and weapons will soon be put to the test.

Matteo, have the legionnaires move out to the crest of the hill. Now sound the order to begin firing. Sound the order for the javelins. Now, sound the advance!

The Gauls were stunned by the intensity of the missile barrage coming from nowhere and shocked to see the full size of the force bearing down on them. We were three legions, with over eighty centuries, about to crush them. We reached the outskirts of their camp before many could arm themselves. Those that did quickly gathered to form a line. They began madly screaming, swinging their swords above their heads, yelling their fevered battle cries. Then the order to charge was given, and they rushed up the slope straight at us.

Moments before our lines clashed, Matteo sounded the order to lower the spears. Seconds later, they drove them straight into the charging Gauls. Many were cut down before their long swords could reach us. Those who did batter their way through the rows of spears, only to find their thrashing almost useless, as their blows struck our strengthened shields. Others abandoned their long swords entirely and attempted to dislodge our javelins embedded into their shields. As they labored to remove them, many were quickly cut down.

Matteo sounded the cavalry charge, and they fell in behind us. We charged the field, cut down many running, abandoning the battle.

No one is to escape!

Toscano, those turning are not Senones. They're Etruscans.

They've joined the Gauls and will die with them. We're now Roman and must act like ones.

Tarsus! The battle is lost! Drop your shield and run! Now! Come! Run! Run for the tree line before it's too late.

Tarsus, look out! Behind you!

Tarsus? It's Tarsus, Toscano.

You must finish him. Now!

I can't. I couldn't kill him; he was my friend. I can't.

Matteo, he's gravely injured. It's the only way. Let it be done.

Tarsus, listen, I am going to save you.

Matteo, my old friend, I'm a soldier and chose to die as one. Goodbye, Matteo.

Tarsus! No!

It's done. He's gone, Matteo. He died bravely.
Come, he knew it was his time and did what
had to be done. Come, we must go. The gods
have willed us to live to fight again.

CHAPTER 35: THE PASSAGE

With the threats of external conflicts finally at a pause, the attention of the people of Rome again turned to the balance of power in the Senate. After years of futile struggles to gain a more significant measure of political power, the ordinary people were again united in their demand for a plebeian to be chosen as one consul. With rioting mounting and threats of a succession looming within the populace of Rome, the people appealed to Camillus for his support to quell the uprising and advance the election of a plebian as a consular.

Villa of Marcus Camillus

Toscano, I have news for you, I'm resigning my position as Dictator of Rome.

But, General, you still have almost five months remaining in your term, and much still needs to be done.

I'm nearing my eightieth year, Toscano, and well past time for a good Roman to retire. There'll be others who will rise to take my place, even more capable than I. But first, there are a few last things that I must shepherd before I am ready to leave the service of Rome. And one that involves you.

It is difficult for me to envision any future without you, General.

There's a bright future for you, Toscano, and one for Rome. What I am about to say will help make them both so. Rome, as you know, still has many enemies and will continue to face complex challenges ahead. It will need a strong military leader who can inspire his men and be strategic in battle, a leader who can be trusted with the future of Rome. You are such a leader, Toscano. Upon my resignation, I have planned for you to be named Military Tribune. You'll be the new leader of our army and man of the people. All will soon see why I have this faith in you. For the first time, I have also arranged for one of the two consuls of Rome to be a plebeian. Lucius Sextus Lateranus will be chosen as such, with Marcus Aemilius elected as consul from the patricians. With these moves in place, the unrest will be subdued, and my service to Rome will be concluded. I will retire, leaving Rome in peace. You, Toscano Flavius, will ensure that my sacrifices in the service of Rome will not have been in vain.

General, what you have done for Rome will undoubtedly be remembered. I am honored by your faith in me and will proudly serve Rome according to your plans. General, I owe you the greatest of debts, and you have inspired me since the first day we met.

Thank you, Centurion. Now go. If all of this is to go as planned, there is still much that I need to do.

The Rostra

Senators, citizens, and people of Rome, give me your attention. In honor of our great leader, defender, and champion of Rome, the great Marcus Furius Camillus, and for his many victories and conquest over the Gauls, ensuring Rome's continual prosperity and to never forget all he has done in his many years in the service of Rome, I, Lucius Sextus Lateranus, in the name of the god Jupiter, hereby propose, and call on your support to commemorate all these enormous achievements by hosting the *Ludi Capitolini Games.* In his honor, these games will be held on Campus Martius, beginning October fifteenth, and continuing for the next sixteen days. Further, these same celebrations are held every four years in perpetuity.

Villa Solaris

Father, can you take me with you to the games? I can't wait to see the boxing and wrestling. That's what you did, right, father? Papa says so, and he's been teaching Nico and me.

Donato, that was a long time ago, but yes, I trained as a wrestler and boxer when I wasn't much older than you, and Papa made that happen.

When can we go, father? And can Papa, Nico, and Uncle Matteo, all of us, can we go? The champion fighter, Sostratus of Sicyon, will be there. He is the champion of the Isthmian Games, father, and is here to prepare for the Olympic games next month.

How do you know about him and these games?

It was on a poster in the market. Aunt Vera told me. She said he would fight on May thirtieth at the Circus Maximus. Please, father, can we go?

We'll let us see how your mother feels about this.

Now, what's Papa been teaching you?

He's been teaching Nico and me how to wrestle.

Well then, come here and show me what you've learned.

Campus Martius

Look, the wrestlers, father. Can we see them? Nico, look, do you see them?

Donato, slow down. This crowd is enormous, and you could get lost. I don't think your mother and Aunt Vera would be too happy if we came home without you two.

Toscano? Is that you?

Cutu, praise the gods! I thought I might see you here. You're still at it after all these years.

Why, of course, I'm too old to do anything else. And look at you, a Roman Tribune. You were always way too bright for just the arena. And this must be your father, Lucien. Good to see you again, Lucien.

Good to see you also, Cutu. You still look like you're ready for the arena yourself.

With this batch of athletics, I wouldn't last five minutes wrestling any of them.

It looks like you will be putting on quite a spectacle here.

It will be, but not as spectacular as when we met at the Fanum Voltumnae. Those were the days. And remember how spectacular those events were. We made those crowds erupt with excitement.

Yes, I remember, and I also remember you, who opened my eyes to a side of Toscano that I didn't see.

Yes, he has the desire that few own, even back then. I'm sorry he got away. And who may I ask is this?

Cutu, this is my new brother, Matteo.

Centurion, it's a pleasure to meet you. I'm in such good company today. And who are these two young citizens, may I ask?

Cutu, may I introduce my son Donato and his cousin Nico? Say hello to Cutu, boys. He's the best trainer in all of Etruria.

And now you can add Latium to that, also.

Hello sir, can you be our trainer, like you were my father's?

Hold on, Donato, you two are too young to start training.

If I may, Tribune, I started with you when you were not much older than your boy here, if you remember.

Please, father!

Father, can you take the boys to the magician's tent so we can chat privately with Cutu? We'll join you shortly.

What do you think, Matteo?

It may not be such a bad idea, but with all our traveling, it would be good for the boys to learn some skills from him.

Give me a moment to chat with him. I'll come and join you at the magician's tent shortly.

So Cutu, how long has it been eight years?

More like ten.

Well, tell me, how are you doing? Your school? Your champions? And how many treasuries have you emptied recently?

Times have been good to me, Toscano. Particularly good lately. This crop of champions is among the strongest I've ever had. And this Sostratus of Sicyon, he's as good as you could have been.

I'm sure he's even better and making you rich.

Well, yes, we're both doing fine, but I wouldn't mind a little break. I could use a rest from all this traveling. Once these games are done, I was thinking of staying here in Rome for a while, enjoying all it has to offer. Engaging in some private tutoring will fit in nicely if you agree. And it will be suitable for the boys. We can also catch up on old times. What do you say, Tribune?

Always thinking, aren't you, Cutu? Come by my villa tomorrow evening. We will speak more about this; it's on Capitoline Hill.

Oh, I will find you, Tribune. Why don't you let me have the boys meet Sostratus? I'm sure they'd be excited to meet him.

I'm sure they will. Come, we'll ask them.

Villa Solaris

Gia, I just received some sad news, the great
General has died, another victim of this
horrid plague ravaging the city.

Oh, I am so sorry to hear that, Toscano. He
was a fierce leader and an inspiration to all of
Rome. You have lost a loyal friend and
teacher, Toscano.

He was, and more to me.

What will you do now?

He would've liked to continue to serve Rome
as Military Tribune. But now under Publius
Albus. He was recently named dictator of
Rome by the Senate, fearing the latest reports
on the Gauls.

Are the Gauls threatening Rome once more?

There are terrifying reports that the Gauls
have returned and joined with the Volscians,
looting and burning entire villages in the
Anio Valley. They must be dealt with quickly,
or Rome will have no harvest this fall. The
Senate has called for new legions to be
enrolled, and we are leaving for battle in a
week.

Oh, my gods, again, war with the Gauls.

Yes, but this will be the last with them. I will drive them back over the Apennines for good.

Anio Valley, Twenty Miles Northeast of Rome

General, our scouts have found the Gauls. They're camped near the River Anio, with their backs to the Via Salaria bridge.

What do the reports have of their size and encampment, Tribune?

Their camp is not yet fully fortified, General. They're not expecting us to be on them so soon.

What do you suggest we do, Tribune?

General, if we deploy a small company of men under cover of darkness, they may be able to remain undetected and dismantle a path through their unfinished defenses. We launch our attack just before dawn, surprising them before they rise and overrun their camp.

It's a good plan, Tribune. Prepare the men. We will proceed as you describe and annihilate them all. No, Gaul is to get away.

Yes, General.

Matteo, gather a small company of men, and tonight, after midnight, we'll move out to the far corner of their camp, away from their fires. We will remove enough of their barricade to allow at least three abreast to pass. Matteo, this must be done quietly, and we must silence any guard nearby who may discover us before he can alert their camp. When done, we'll return to our lines here and, just before dawn, launch our attack.

Understood, Commander.

It's time. Now we go, and may the gods be pleased.

The Gallic Camp on the River Anio

It's a complete rout, General. We are chasing the remnants trying to flee across the River Anio, but there is a massive barbarian on the River Anio bridge. He is single-handedly holding back our pursuit. He is making a stand there, General, challenging us to single-man combat.

Tribune, ask for a volunteer to come forward to face.

We have a volunteer, General.

Who is this man? I must meet him.

It is I, General. I will fight him.

No, Toscano, I will not allow it. I will not risk losing you as my Tribune. You are too valuable to Rome and me. We will let the barbarian wait there; he cannot stand there forever.

Tribune, we have a volunteer.

Bring him to me, Centurion.

What is your name, legionnaire?

Titus Manlius, Commander.

Titus Manlius, you bring great honor to Rome. Come, we shall bring your request to the General.

General, may I present the legionnaire who has volunteered to combat the barbarian Titus Manlius.

Titus Manlius, it is an honor to meet you. You will bring great praise to your family and will earn the admiration of all of Rome for what you are about to do. Now, go and slay that barbarian. Mars Ultor!

I will, General. Mars Ultor!

Hail Titus! Hail Titus! Hail Titus!

Do you hear that, Matteo?

He has done it! All of Rome will celebrate his victory.

Hail Titus! Hail Titus! Hail Titus!

Sound the charge! We must finish them all now!

Campus Martius

Titus Manlius, for your bravery in single combat at the Battle of River Anio, I Publius Albus Capitolinus, as Dictator of Rome, hereby confer the agnomen onto you and all your descendants, the name of Imperiosus Torquatus. Good to you! Titus Manlius Imperiosus Torquatus!

Hail Titus! Hail Titus! Hail Titus!

Villa Solaris

Toscano, Matteo, come to the gardens. Father has gifts for you both.

Tribune and Centurion, in honor of your military promotions, the boys and I have gifts for both of you. Go ahead, Donato, give this one to your father.

Here, father, Papa made it for you, and I helped him.

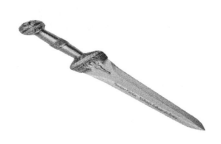

What do we have here, a dagger? It's magnificent. Look at this craftsmanship. Thank you, father.

Look at the engraving on the other side of the blade.

"Toscano Flavius - Militaris Tribune de Roma,"

Such fine work. It's magnificent. Thank you, Father.

Here Nico, give this one to your father.

Just look at this. It's remarkable work. And look at this engraving.

*"Res of Matteo Fremitus Lupi -
Centurion Primus Pilus de Roma."*

*(Property Of Matteo, the Growling Wolf-
First Centurion of Rome.)*

And this wolf looks impressive. I will wear it with honor. Thank you, Father.

Can I hold it?

Be careful, Nico. It's very sharp.

Are you part wolf, Father?

No, but some people say I growl like one
when I aim my bow.

Can I hear it, Father?

Yes, uncle, can we hear you?

Well, I need a bow. I'll pretend to have my
bow. Let's see; I'm pulling back the string,
aiming, and Grrrrrrrgh.

That does sound like a growl, uncle. You're
part wolf.

Tribune Flavius and Centurion Lupi, come.
Dinner is waiting.

Tribune, I heard about the new Titus Manlius
Imperiosus Torquatus being named Dictator
yesterday. Do you think Rome confuses him
with his uncle?

Well, that name does come with much
history.

It certainly does, and I don't think we've
heard the last from this Manlius.

Neither do I.

And I wouldn't be surprised if it's much
sooner than we think.

Made in the USA
Monee, IL
30 October 2024

69009916R10193